New English Master
リーディングにつなげる英文法

by
Nagaki Kitayama
Margaret Yamanaka
Keiichiro Fukui

Photographs by
@iStockphoto.com
Getty Images
Denis Lalor

音声ファイルのダウンロード／ストリーミング

CD マーク表示がある箇所は、音声を弊社 HP より無料でダウンロード／ストリーミングすることができます。トップページのバナーをクリックし、書籍検索してください。書籍詳細ページに音声ダウンロードアイコンがございますのでそちらから自習用音声としてご活用ください。

https://www.seibido.co.jp

New English Master

Copyright © 2016 by Nagaki Kitayama, Margaret Yamanaka, Keiichiro Fukui

*All rights reserved for Japan.
No part of this book may be reproduced in any form
without permission from Seibido Co., Ltd.*

はじめに

本テキストの目標とねらい

　New English Master は基本英文法とエッセイ・リーディングを組み合わせた総合英語教材で、*Mastering Basic English Grammar, English Makeover* の続編です。文法解説は学習者の皆さんに負担の少ない例文を使い簡潔な説明に努めました。英文読解は異文化理解に必要な話題を豊富にそろえました。基本英文法を理解し英文を読む力をつけることを目標とします。そして、英語というツールを活用して皆さんの視野が広がることをねらいとします。

本テキストの構成と内容

　本テキストは、基本英文法の解説と練習、そして英文読解とリスニング練習により、初級・中級者の総合的な英語力を向上させることを目標に作成しました。全26課で各レッスンは4ページです。前半の見開き2ページは英文理解のための文法解説とその練習問題、後半の2ページはエッセイ・リーディングとその内容把握問題の構成となっています。

　各レッスンの文法解説の最後に文法理解の確認のための《チェックテスト》を設けました。《チェックテスト》は学習者の文法理解度を測るための予習用にも活用できます。文法理解を定着させるための練習問題の出題形式は、空所補充、書き換え、誤文訂正、和訳、文法説明、並べ替え問題等、学習者になじみのあるオーソドックスなものにしてあります。また、練習問題は前ページの文法解説と完全対応していますので、中級レベルのクラスでは個人学習による予習が充分にできるようになっています。

　READING PASSAGE の英文は全て250語程度のオリジナルエッセイです。学習者にとって常識として知ってもらいたいスタンダードなテーマとなっています。取り上げた人物は、ノーベル平和賞受賞者のマララさん、アップル社のジョブズ氏、シャーロックホームズ、チャップリン、ガーフィールド。扱った国は、シンガポール、エジプト、オーストラリア、中国、アフリカ。そして、多くの人が注目するトピックとして、食品、健康、音楽、農業、インターネット、言語などです。また、身近な生活の様子を描写したエッセイもあります。英文を読んだ後、学生個人が興味を持った内容をさらに深く追求できるように工夫してあります。

　英文読解の理解と応用のために、**NOTES** では語彙項目の解説、**STORY BANK** は内容確認のための正誤問題です。**CULTURAL BANK** は英文の内容の発展理解と異文化理解を深めるための内容をディクテーション形式で学習します。そして **GRAMMAR BANK** はエッセイ・リーディングの内容と当該文法項目の総合演習となっています。

　最後になりましたが、本書の作成にあたっては株式会社成美堂の松本健治氏、佐藤公雄氏に多大な労を取っていただきました。ここに感謝の意を表します。

2015年
猛暑の70年、夏

著者一同

CONTENTS

Lesson	Grammar	Reading	Page
Lesson 1	名詞	*It's a Long Way to the Top*	2
Lesson 2	冠詞	*Singapore's Chingay Parade*	6
Lesson 3	代名詞(1)	*English, for Better or for Worse*	10
Lesson 4	代名詞(2)	*How Important Is Education to You*	14
Lesson 5	時制	*From Anime to Zen*	18
Lesson 6	進行形	*The Storm*	22
Lesson 7	完了形(1)	*Public Works for the State and the Citizens*	26
Lesson 8	完了形(2)	*Riding an Old Steam Train*	30
Lesson 9	助動詞(1)	*Farm Stays*	34
Lesson 10	助動詞(2)	*Is Sunshine Really Bad for Us?*	38
Lesson 11	関係詞(1)	*What's in a Name?*	42
Lesson 12	関係詞(2)	*You Are What You Eat*	46
Lesson 13	態(1)	*A Car for the Blind?*	50
Lesson 14	態(2)	*Talking Drums*	54
Lesson 15	不定詞(1)	*The Future for Farmers*	58
Lesson 16	不定詞(2)	*The Extraordinary Steve Jobs*	62
Lesson 17	分詞(1)	*A Cool Memory*	66
Lesson 18	分詞(2)	*Holmes? Watson?*	70
Lesson 19	動名詞(1)	*Aussie English*	74
Lesson 20	動名詞(2)	*Garfield*	78
Lesson 21	形容詞・副詞	*Climbing*	82
Lesson 22	比較(1)	*Lost in Translation*	86
Lesson 23	比較(2)	*Preservatives*	90
Lesson 24	前置詞	*The Tramp*	94
Lesson 25	仮定法(1)	*Presenting Successfully*	98
Lesson 26	仮定法(2)	*"What if…"*	102

LESSON 1　　　　　　　　　　名　詞

◆ A. 数えられる名詞

(1) **普通名詞** (boy, dog, chair, lake, week, *etc.*)：同種類に属する個々のものを表す名詞で、単数形と複数形とがある。

　1. My **daughter** is ten **years** old.
　2. There is a **picture** on the **wall**.

(2) **集合名詞** (class, family, audience, team, people, *etc.*)：人や物の集合体を表す名詞で、次の2つの用法がある。

　3. a. My **family** *is* a large one.　　　　　　　　　　　　〈集合体〉
　　 b. My **family** *are* all well.　　　　　　　　　　　　　〈構成員〉

◆ B. 数えられない名詞

(1) **固有名詞** (Richard, Paris, America, Nagoya Station, *etc.*)：特定の人・物・場所などを表す名詞で、必ず大文字で書き始める。

　1. **Mr. Johnson** takes **the Japan Times**.
　2. **Japan** is in the east of **Asia**.

(2) **物質名詞** (milk, bread, medicine, salt, gold, fire, *etc.*)：物質や材料を表す名詞で、常に単数形で用いられる。

　3. Cows supply us with **milk**.
　4. Give me *two sheets of* **paper**.
　☞ その他：*a cup of* tea, *a sheet of* paper, *a cake of* soap, *a bottle of* beer, *a slice of* bread, *a spoonful of* sugar, *etc.*

(3) **抽象名詞** (beauty, peace, honesty, success, advice, *etc.*)：性質・動作・状態などの抽象概念を表す名詞で、常に単数形で用いられる。

　5. Do you believe in **life** after **death**?
　6. Hard work is the key to **success**.

《チェックテスト1》

次の各文の名詞に下線を引き、その種類を言いなさい。
　1. He takes some medicine every morning.
　2. She brought me a glass of water.
　3. I asked the doctor for his advice.
　4. There are five members in my family.

EXERCISE 1

〈1〉次の各文の( )から適切なものを選びなさい。

1. Do you like (a tomato / tomatoes)?
2. Deborah has short black (hair / hairs).
3. I'll give you some (advice / advices).
4. Two (family / families) live in the same house.
5. Our class (is / are) made up of 35 students.
6. There (was / were) a large audience in the concert hall.

〈2〉( )内の日本語を英語に変えて、次の各文を完成しなさい。

1. I drink (2杯の) coffee every day.

2. He eats (2枚の) bread for breakfast.

3. There was (1本の) milk in the fridge.

4. She bought (3個の) soap at K's Mart.

〈3〉次の各文の意味を書きなさい。

1. A four-leaf clover is a symbol of good luck.

2. The audience were all excited by the magic show.

3. There are four pieces of furniture in this room.

4. Tobacco is more injurious to our health than alcohol.

〈4〉次の各文の( )内の語を並べ替えて正しい文にしなさい。

1. The city (south / in / of / the / is / England).

2. She put (tea / a / of / her / sugar / spoonful / in).

3. There were (people / conference / at / 80 / the / about).

READING PASSAGE 1

It's a Long Way to the Top

Motonari Ono is a budding fashion designer. He has held shows in India, Indonesia, and Hong Kong, and will go to (1)Russia next season. He is one of many young designers based in Tokyo. Young designers like Ono are trying to enter both the Japanese and international fashion scenes.

After graduating from a local fashion college in 2002, Ono went overseas. He spent a total of four years abroad. First, he attended the London College of Fashion, and then he studied at the Royal Academy of Fine Arts in Belgium. Then he met Bora Aksu, a successful Turkish-born (2)designer.

Soon Ono was back in London making patterns for the Aksu brand. Ono also designed some clothes himself. He says that he got invaluable (3)advice from Aksu. "Learning on the job is so much better than just learning from a textbook," he says.

Ono is now producing under his own name brand. He focuses on the 25-35 age (4)group. "I make dresses for women who know quality. These women are usually tired of fast fashion. Fast fashion is like fast food: it all looks the same. It takes time and effort to make good clothes." Yuka, a model, has several of the Ono brand dresses. She says, "They are very feminine. He uses a lot of (5)lace and soft materials that complement me. I feel good, too, when I wear them."

Authenticity is a key word for Ono. "I use only the best," he concludes.

NOTES

budding「新進の」 **based in Tokyo**「東京に本拠を置く」 **local**「地元の」 **the London College of Fashion**「ロンドン・カレッジ・オブ・ファッション」（英国唯一のファッション系大学） **the Royal Academy of Fine Arts**「（アントウェルペン）王立芸術学院」 **Bora Aksu**「ボラアクス」（BORA AKSU：英国のファッションブランド） **Turkish-born**「トルコ生まれの」 **making patterns ＝ and made patterns**「デザインをした」 **invaluable**「きわめて貴重な」 **on the job**「働いて」 **name brand**「ブランド名」 **fast fashion**「ファスト・ファッション」（最新の流行を取り入れた低価格の衣料品） **feminine**「女性らしい、優しい」 **complement~**「～にぴったり合う」 **authenticity**「本物」

STORY BANK

本文の内容と合っているものにはT、間違っているものにはFを書き入れなさい。

(1) (　　) Ono held shows in India and Russia.
(2) (　　) Ono studied at a fashion college in London.
(3) (　　) Ono makes dresses for women with a Turkish designer now.
(4) (　　) The dresses of Ono's brand are made from soft materials and they are fast fashion.

CULTURAL BANK

英文を聞いて空所に適切な語を書き入れなさい。

(1) A designer is a professional who makes (　　　　) or (　　　　　).
(2) An academy is a school for training in a special (　　　　) or (　　　　).
(3) Belgium is in north-western Europe between (　　　　) and (　　　　).
(4) Regent (　　　　) is in central London and is a popular (　　　　) for shopping.

GRAMMAR BANK

本文中の下線部(1)～(5)の名詞の種類を2ページの文法解説を参考に答えなさい。

(1) ＿＿＿＿＿＿＿　(2) ＿＿＿＿＿＿＿　(3) ＿＿＿＿＿＿＿
(4) ＿＿＿＿＿＿＿　(5) ＿＿＿＿＿＿＿

LESSON 2　　　　　　　　　冠　詞

A. 不定冠詞 (a, an) の用法 — 数えられる名詞の単数形の前に付ける。

1. He had **a** book under his arm.　　　　　　　　　　〈漠然と1つのものを指す場合〉
2. **An** ostrich runs very quickly.「～というもの」　　　　　〈種族全体〉
3. I'll stay here for **a** week or two.「1つの」(=one)
4. My brother gets 800 dollars **a** week.「～につき、～ごとに」(=per)
5. **A** woman came to see me yesterday.「ある」(=a certain)

B. 定冠詞 (the) の用法 — どんな種類の名詞にも、また単複の区別なく用いられる。

1. The boy wore a cap. **The** cap was bright blue.〈前出の名詞を繰り返す場合〉
2. **The** earth is a part of **the** universe.　　　　　　　〈ただ1つの物〉
3. Where is **the** bathroom, please?　　　　　　　　　〈周囲の情況から明らかな場合〉
4. He is **the** dean *of the medical school*.　　　　　　　〈句による限定〉
5. **The** tea I like best is from England.　　　　　　　〈節による限定〉
6. **The** lion is a fierce animal.「～というもの」　　　　　〈種族全体〉
7. **The** *young* must be kind to **the** *old*.　　　　　　　〈the+形容詞=「～の人々」〉
8. We sell land by **the** *tsubo*.「坪いくらで」　　　　　　〈単位〉
9. Peter slapped me on **the** face.　　　　　　　　　〈身体の一部〉

C. 冠詞の省略

1. **Waiter**, a cup of coffee, please.　　　　　　　　〈呼びかけ〉
2. **Father** isn't back from town yet.　　　　　　　　〈家族関係〉
3. What time is **school** over?　　　　　　　　　　〈建物などが本来の目的を表す場合〉
4. He was chosen **captain**.　　　　　　　　　　　〈身分・官職を表す語が補語となる場合〉

《チェックテスト2》

次の各文の（　）内に、必要に応じて適切な冠詞を補いなさい。
1. I go to (　) museum once (　) month.
2. She rented (　) house by (　) year.
3. (　) man with (　) black coat is Mike.
4. They appointed him (　) manager of (　) hotel.

EXERCISE 2

〈1〉次の各文の適切な位置に冠詞を補って文を完成しなさい。

1. Dog generally dislikes cat.

2. Moon moves around earth.

3. There was not cloud in sky.

4. He is governor of prefecture.

〈2〉次の各文の誤りを正しなさい。

1. I am studying a life of Columbus.

2. She went to an airport to meet him.

3. Is he the teacher at your school?

4. He was elected the president in 1997.

〈3〉次の各文の意味を書きなさい。

1. In a sense, life is only a dream.

2. My car does 40 miles to the gallon.

3. They provided food and shelter for the poor.

4. She opened the window to get some fresh air.

〈4〉次の各文の(　)内の語を並べ替えて正しい文にしなさい。

1. He (the / a / takes / twice / day / medicine).

2. A sailor (person / works / is / on / a / who / ships).

3. Where (the / which / cellphones / is / sells / store)?

READING PASSAGE 2

Singapore's Chingay Parade

Singapore is a small but economically rich country. It lies at the tip of the Malay Peninsula. Its population is about 5.5 million. This city-state is about the same size as metropolitan Tokyo and covers an area of about 700 square kilometers. (1)The official languages are English, Malay, Mandarin Chinese and Tamil. Everyone speaks more than one language. Singaporeans take pride in their multicultural society. The Chingay Parade is (2)a symbol of that pride.

In February, (3)the people of Singapore come together to celebrate Chinese New Year. Because a large part of the population is Chinese, they used to use firecrackers. They think that firecrackers will frighten away evil spirits. In 1973, the government put a ban on firecrackers, so the then-Prime Minister Lee Kuan Yew suggested a noisy parade instead. The first Chingay Parade was small. Gradually, the parade grew more popular. Now there are more than 11,000 performers.

Each year has a theme. In 2015, the country of Singapore celebrated its 50th year of independence from Britain, so (4)the theme was "We love Singapore." Professionals design some of the floats, but many are hand-made by school children or suburban community groups. It is very exciting. As soon as one year is finished, people start to plan for, and look forward to, the next year's event.

Harmony is very important to Singaporeans. This small country has high taxes, and many restrictions and regulations, but the people work hard together to make it a clean, safe and happy place to live.

NOTES

Singapore「シンガポール」　at the tip of Malay Penisula「マレー半島の先端に」　city-state「都市国家」　metropolitan Tokyo「東京23区」　cover~「~に及ぶ」　official language「公用語」　take pride in~「~を誇りに思う」　multicultural society「多文化社会」　Chingay Parade「チンゲイ・パレード」　Chinese New Year「春節」（旧正月）　firecracker「爆竹」　frighten away evil spirits「邪気を追い払う、魔よけ」　put a ban on~「~を禁止する」　then-Prime Minister Lee Kuan Yew「当時の首相リー・クアンユー」　professional「専門家」　float「山車（だし）」　suburban「郊外の」　restriction「制限」　regulation「規則」

STORY BANK

本文の内容と合っているものにはT、間違っているものにはFを書き入れなさい。

(1) (　) Singapore is a very small but rich country.
(2) (　) People now use firecrackers at the Chingay Parade to frighten evil spirits away.
(3) (　) Some floats are made by professionals and others are made by non-professionals.
(4) (　) Many people live in the small country of Singapore, and there are many restrictions and regulations there.

CULTURAL BANK

英文を聞いて空所に適切な語を書き入れなさい。

(1) Mandarin Chinese is (　　　　) official language of both China and Taiwan, and also one of the (　　　　) official languages of Singapore.
(2) (　　　　) (　　　　) day of Chinese New Year falls between January 21 and February 20.
(3) Lee Kuan Yew was (　　　　) prime minister of Singapore from 1959 to 1990 and became the (　　　　) serving prime minister in world history.
(4) During Lee's long rule, Singapore became (　　　　) (　　　　) prosperous nation in Southeast Asia.

GRAMMAR BANK

本文中の下線部(1)～(4)の冠詞の用法を、6ページの文法解説を参考に答えなさい。

(1) _____　(2) _____　(3) _____　(4) _____

LESSON 3　　　　　代名詞 (1)

◆ A. 「一般の人々」を表す we, you, they

1. **We** have many rainy days in June.
2. **You** never know what will happen.
3. **They** say that he is a billionaire.

◆ B. it の特別用法

1. **It**'s five past seven now. 〈時間〉
2. **It**'s very cold today, isn't it? 〈天候〉
3. **It**'s about three miles to Boston. 〈距離〉
4. **It**'s quite dark in the hall. 〈明暗〉
5. **It**'s dangerous *to swim in this pond*. 〈形式主語〉
6. I found **it** easy *to solve the problem*. 〈形式目的語〉

◆ C. this と that

1. **This** is a desk and **that** is a table. 〈近い物と遠い物〉
2. His *manner* is not **that** of a gentleman. 〈名詞の繰り返し〉
3. Her *eyes* are like **those** of a leopard.
4. *Sam is too selfish.* **That**'s why I dislike him. 〈前述の文の内容〉
5. I know **this**: *she knows a lot about cars*. 〈後述の文の内容〉

◆ D. 再帰代名詞 — 語尾が -self, -selves で終わる代名詞をいう。

(1) **再帰用法**：動詞・前置詞の目的語となる。
　　1. Did you enjoy **yourself** at the party?
(2) **強意用法**：名詞・代名詞と同格に用いて、それらの意味を強調する。
　　2. Have some cake. I made it **myself**.

《チェックテスト3》

次の各文の(　)内に適切な代名詞を補いなさい。
1. (　　　) have a lot of snow in Akita.
2. The boy hid (　　　) in the closet.
3. Her feelings were (　　　) of a little girl.
4. I can tell you (　　　): he did not die of an illness.

EXERCISE 3

① 次の各文中の it が何を表しているか指摘しなさい。
1. It is ten past seven by my watch. (　　　　)
2. It is not good to eat between meals. (　　　　)
3. How far is it from here to Kanazawa? (　　　　)
4. I think it our duty to help the weak. (　　　　)
5. Where is the stapler? Have you seen it? (　　　　)

② 次の各文の(　)内に適切な再帰代名詞を補いなさい。
1. I enjoyed (　　　　) at the festival.
2. My daughter can now dress (　　　　).
3. He cut (　　　　) while he was shaving.
4. The cat is licking (　　　　) with its tongue.

③ 日本文の意味を表すように、次の各文の(　)内に適語を補いなさい。
1. ブラジルでは何語を話しますか。
   What language (　　　　) (　　　　) speak in Brazil?
2. 英国の面積は日本の面積よりも小さい。
   The area of Britain is smaller than (　　　　) (　　　　) Japan.

④ 次の各文の意味を書きなさい。
1. They say that it is bad luck to spill salt.

2. I know this: she was killed by someone in the woods.

3. The pears in the box are better than those in the basket.

⑤ 次の各文の(　)内の語を並べ替えて正しい文にしなさい。
1. We (four / in / have / year / seasons / a).

2. I found (climb / it / that / difficult / tree / to).

3. It is (to / the / you / doctor / necessary / see / for).

READING PASSAGE 3

English, for Better or for Worse

What's happening to English? English is expanding into a global language. Millions of people all over the world use it every day. (1)They say that English is changing because of the internet. That's not good, or is it? Many students depend on computer software to check their grammar and spelling. Is (2)that because they can't read or write English anymore? Some scholars think so.

Other scholars, however, disagree. They say that the internet is a boon for English. Now (3)it is easy to write in English; telephone text messages, e-mails, Facebook updates, Twitter posts, blogs and even e-books. Writers come from all over the world. And so do their audiences.

We can help ourselves get better at writing by reading books. In fact, along with the increase in "writers" who want to write well, there is a sudden increase in the number of books on themes such as grammar and punctuation. These books are not like those we used in primary school or high school. They read like an entertaining story book.

Take *You Send Me*, for example. This book explains how to write an e-mail that is clear, and reads well. *Origin of the Specious* looks at the differences between British English and American English. Did you know that the American version is often the older version of a word? *Eats, Shoots & Leaves* shows us some of the funny punctuation mistakes (4)we make.

One expert, Douglas Harper, says this about writing and the internet: The "right way" to use a word is the one that communicates your ideas best.

NOTES

for better or for worse「善かれ悪しかれ」 **expand**「発展する」 **global**「世界的規模の」 **boon (for)**「(〜にとり)恩恵」 **so do~**「〜もそうである」 **help oneself get better at writing**「自分で努力して書くことがより上手になる」 **along with~**「〜に加えて」 **(book) on~**「〜についての(本)」 **punctuation**「句読点」 **primary school**「小学校」 **entertaining**「面白い」 **story book**「物語の本」 **an e-mail...reads well**「読みやすい電子メール」 **the specious**「見かけのよい人」 **version** = English

STORY BANK

本文の内容と合っているものにはT、間違っているものにはFを書き入れなさい。

(1) (　) We can say that English is a global language because people use computer software to check their English.

(2) (　) Some scholars disagree with the comment that students can't read or write English because of computers.

(3) (　) Now, there are many interesting books on grammar and punctuation.

(4) (　) One expert says that the "right way" to use a word means using words without any mistakes.

CULTURAL BANK

07

英文を聞いて空所に適切な語を書き入れなさい。

(1) Stickers or (　　　　) are an important feature of LINE and can express more than (　　　).

(2) *You Send Me* reminds (　　) of Sam Cooke and (　　) famous song *Wonderful World*.

(3) Darwin (　　　) developed the theory of evolution and wrote about (　　　) ideas in the book *On the Origin of Species* in 1859.

(4) (　　　) saw a sign saying *Eats, Shoots & Leaves*. It was supposed to tell (　　) that "The panda eats shoots and leaves."

【shoots「若芽」(パンダの餌)】

GRAMMAR BANK

本文中の下線部(1)〜(4)の代名詞の用法を、10ページの文法解説を参考に答えなさい。

(1) ＿＿＿＿＿　(2) ＿＿＿＿＿　(3) ＿＿＿＿＿　(4) ＿＿＿＿＿

LESSON 4　　　　代名詞 (2)

A. 再帰代名詞を含む慣用表現

1. I went to the movies **by myself**.「一人で」(=alone)
2. He cooked a big meal **for himself**.「自分のために、独力で」
3. The search for truth is good **in itself**.「それ自体」

B. 不定代名詞 ― 不定数量を表す代名詞で、その多くは形容詞としても用いられる。不定代名詞と動詞の数(すう)に注意。

1. **One** should do one's [his] duty. 《文語》　　　　　〈一般の人々〉
2. If you want an eraser, I'll lend you **one**.　　　　　〈不特定の物〉
   Cf. If you want this eraser, I'll lend **it** to you.　　〈特定の物〉
3. Are there **any** eggs in the fridge? ― Yes. there are **some**.
   Cf. Will you buy me **some** doughnuts?
      (=Please buy me some doughnuts.)
4. I have two dogs. **One** is brown, and **the other** is white. 〈もう一方の物〉
5. This shirt is too small. Show me **another**.　　　　　〈別の1つ〉
6. **Each** of them *was* given a present.「めいめい」
7. **Each** bedroom *has* its own shower.「それぞれの」　　〈形容詞〉
8. **Every** child *likes* toys.「すべての」　　　　　　　　〈形容詞〉
9. **Both** of us *are* movie fans.「両方」
10. **Both** (the) women *are* nurses.「2人とも」　　　　　〈形容詞〉
11. Do you know **either** of the brothers?「(～のうちの)どちらか」
12. There are roses on **either** side of the door.「どちらの～も」〈形容詞〉
13. **Neither** of the roads *is* [*are*] very good.「...のどちらも～ない」
14. **Neither** window *faces* the sea.「どちらの...も～ない」〈形容詞〉

《チェックテスト4》

次の各文の( )内から適切なものを選びなさい。
1. (Either / Both) of them are still alive.
2. Every flower (have / has) its own smell.
3. I have lost my pen. I must buy (it / one).
4. Neither book (is / are) very helpful to me.

EXERCISE 4

〈①〉次の各文の（　）内に、下記の語群から適語を選んで補いなさい。
1. (　　) of the two answers is correct.
2. (　　) country has its own customs.
3. One pole is long and the (　　) pole is short.
4. (　　) men are computer engineers.
5. There are trees on (　　) side of the street.
6. This jacket is too small. Please show me (　　).
   [another / both / either / every / neither / other]

〈②〉日本文の意味を表すように、次の各文の（　）内に適語を補いなさい。
1. その小説のどちらかを読んだことがありますか。
   Have you ever read (　　) (　　) the novels?
2. 人間の性質は本来おだやかなものではない。
   Human nature is not gentle (　　) (　　).
3. 彼女はその分譲マンションに一人で住んでいる。
   She lives all (　　) (　　) in the condominium.

〈③〉次の各文の意味を書きなさい。
1. Both of my friends are interested in gardening.

2. There were two doors at either end of the hall.

3. I shook hands with each member of the soccer team.

4. Is there any soda left in the bottle? — Yes, there is some.

〈④〉次の各文の（　）内の語を並べ替えて正しい文にしなさい。
1. Neither (a / us / card / had / of / credit).

2. Each (the / likes / of / futsal / boys / playing).

3. Every (in / has / house / sold / this / been / street).

READING PASSAGE 4

How Important Is Education to You

Carl and Hideo have two things in common. Neither of them has any higher education. (1)<u>Both</u> of them wanted to go to university. Carl finished at the end of junior high school. Then he went to work for a mechanic. Hideo finished at the end of senior high school. Then he went to work for an electrician.

(2)<u>Both</u> men had to work to help their families. (3)<u>Each</u> of them is happy with their job, but neither of them can give up the hope of one day going back to school.

Yukie also had to finish school early. She had always wanted to go on to university and get a degree. She believes that everyone should follow their dream. Her husband agreed. "If you want a university degree, get (4)<u>one</u>," he said. So she did. For 25 years she saved a little money (5)<u>each</u> year, then she became a freshman the same year her son did. Now she is a home economics teacher.

Many young people value education, but can't go to school. But the United Nations tries to bring education to all children of all nations. At the head of this movement now is Malala Yousafzai. Malala is one person who will never give up the fight for education. In 2012, she was shot because she went to school. She survived, and now she wants to tell everyone that education is the only way to change the world. There is now a Malala Day. On Malala Day, young people join together and discuss how they can improve education worldwide.

"One child, one teacher, one pen and one book can change the world," she says.

NOTES

in common「共通な」　**higher education**「高等教育」　**junior high school**「中学校」
senior high school「高校」　**go back to school**「学校に戻る」　**degree**「学位」
home economics「家庭科(の)」　**value~**「~に価値を置く」　**the United Nations**
= the U.N.「国際連合」　**at the head of~**「~の先頭・代表に」　**Malala Yousafzai**
「マララ・ユスフザイ」(史上最年少のノーベル平和賞受賞者、パキスタン人)
she was shot「彼女は銃撃された」　**worldwide**「世界的に」

STORY BANK

本文の内容と合っているものにはT、間違っているものにはFを書き入れなさい。

(1) (　) Carl became a mechanic after finishing junior high school.
(2) (　) Hideo became an electrician after finishing college.
(3) (　) Although Yukie's husband was against the idea, she got a university degree.
(4) (　) Malala said, "One child, one teacher, one pen and one book can change the world."

CULTURAL BANK　　　　　　　　　　　　　　　　　　　　　　　09

英文を聞いて空所に適切な語を書き入れなさい。

(1) The United Nations is an international organization and (　　　　) headquarters are in New York City. Almost every country in the world belongs to (　　　　).
(2) "Education is the (　　　　) solution. (　　　　) child, one teacher, one pen and one (　　　　) can change the world," said Malala.
(3) "The pen is mightier than the sword," means that communication is a more effective tool (　　　　) (　　　　) than direct violence.
(4) In Japan, (　　　　) child between the ages of 6 and 14 has to go to school and (　　　　).

GRAMMAR BANK

本文中の下線部(1)~(5)の品詞(不定代名詞か形容詞)を答えなさい。

(1) _____　(2) _____　(3) _____　(4) _____
(5) _____

LESSON 5　　　　　時制

◇A. 現在時制 ― 現在時を表す動詞の形。
　(1) 現在の事実・状態を表す。
　　1. She **is** a university student.
　(2) 現在の習慣的・反復的動作を表す。
　　2. I usually **get** home at about seven.
　(3) 時に関係のない一般的真理を表す。
　　3. Water **boils** at 100 degrees centigrade.
　(4) 未来の確定した予定・計画を表す。
　　4. My aunt **comes** here tomorrow afternoon.

◇B. 過去時制 ― 過去時を表す動詞の形。
　(1) 過去の動作・状態を表す。
　　1. He once **had** a large company in New York.
　(2) 過去の習慣的・反復的動作を表す。
　　2. We sometimes **played** tennis after school.

◇C. 未来時制 ― 未来時を表す動詞の形。
　(1) 単純未来：意志を含まない、単なる未来の出来事を表す。
　　1. I **will** [**shall**] be 20 next year.［shall は主に《英》］
　(2) 意志未来：平叙文では主語や話し手の意志を表し、疑問文では聞き手の意思を尋ねるのに用いられる。
　　2. I **will** lend you this comic book.「～しましょう」
　　3. The window **won't** open.「どうしても～しない」[**won't**=will not]
　　4. **Shall** I make coffee for you?「～しましょうか」
　　5. **Will** you phone me later, please?「～してくださいませんか」

《チェックテスト5》

> 次の各文の現在時制の用法は、A.(1)～(4)のどれに当たりますか。
> 1. We often go on picnics by bicycle.
> 2. Five and seven make(s) twelve.
> 3. The church stands on a low hill.
> 4. The ship sails for Kobe this evening.

EXERCISE 5

⟨①⟩ 次の各文の(　)内の動詞を適切な形に変えなさい。

1. I (send) him an email yesterday.　　　(　　　　　)
2. Light (travel) faster than sound.　　　(　　　　　)
3. The town (lie) east of the river.　　　(　　　　　)
4. George (be) idle when he was young.　　　(　　　　　)

⟨②⟩ 次の各文の(　)内に will または shall を補いなさい。

1. He (　　　) surely win the half marathon.
2. What restaurant (　　　) we go to?
3. (　　　) you show me your new tablet?
4. (　　　) I introduce Mrs. Yokoyama to you?

⟨③⟩ 次の各文の誤りを正しなさい。

1. An elephant had a long trunk.

2. Angela sometimes visit her aunt.

3. I hope it is fine weather tomorrow.

⟨④⟩ 次の各文の意味を書きなさい。

1. The Seine flows through the middle of Paris.

2. The drugstore opens at 9:00 a.m. and closes at 10:00 p.m..

3. How long will it take if you walk to the aquarium?

⟨⑤⟩ 次の各文の(　)内の語を並べ替えて正しい文にしなさい。

1. He (be / says / tomorrow / will / busy / he).

2. She (to / at / usually / bed / eleven / goes).

3. I know (any / won't / me / that / money / he / lend).

READING PASSAGE 5

From Anime to Zen

Are you an otaku? Early in July, Paris holds its annual Japan Expo. About 3,000 people attended the first Japan Expo in 1999, but now more than 240,000 people attend. Anime and manga fans sometimes arrive in cosplay outfits, imitating their favorite character.

"Sailor Moon" and "Dragon Ball" costumes are popular. There once was a young French lady dressed exactly like a *maiko*, too. Besides the many booths for people interested in manga, video games, figures and other anime stuff, there are also booths for people who like ikebana and Zen. You can even experience shiatsu for just five euros.

The popularity of Japanese things amazes Japanese artists who visit, and so does the use of many Japanese words. It will not surprise you to hear that Japanism has influenced European Art since the 19th century. Then in the 1970s, Japanese animated films became popular there.

The interest in art and entertainment led to an interest in some Japanese words, such as "kabuki," "ukiyo-e," and "origami." In fact, there are now over 100 Japanese words in the Oxford English Dictionary. Some words will shock you. There is "karoshi," "hikikomori," "zaibatsu," and even "bento." Some are new additions to the dictionary, but some entered the English language more than a hundred years ago.

How do words get added to a dictionary? New words will get added if they are used often by many people in many different fields. It usually takes two or three years of research. So, will a word like "*matcha*" get added? Possibly. But you will find "cha" there already.

NOTES

hold~「~を開催する」 **annual**「年に一度の」 **cosplay** ＝ **costume** ＋ **play**「コスプレ」 **booth**「（展示会場の）ブース」 **figure**「フィギュア」 **stuff**「もの」 **euro**「（通貨）ユーロ」 **amaze~**「~をびっくりさせる」 **Japanism**「日本風、日本趣味」 **animated film**「アニメ映画」 **the Oxford English Dictionary** ＝ **OED**『オックスフォード英語辞典』 **addition**「（辞書項目への）追加」

STORY BANK

本文の内容と合っているものにはT、間違っているものにはFを書き入れなさい。

(1) (　) Japan Expo had only a few visitors in the beginning, but now there are many.
(2) (　) In the Japan Expo, there are some booths for people who like traditional things.
(3) (　) Japanese things are popular in Paris recently, but were not so a long time ago.
(4) (　) We can say that "karoshi," "gaijin," "zaibatsu" and "bento" are English words.

CULTURAL BANK

英文を聞いて空所に適切な語を書き入れなさい。

(1) A Japanese research institute (　　　　) otaku into twelve groups and (　　　　) the size and market impact of each of these groups.
(2) *Maiko* (　　　　) green tea and *dango* to people at teahouses in the temple town of Kyoto about 300 years (　　　　).
(3) Every euro coin (　　　　) a common European face. On the head side, each member state (　　　　) the coins with their own motifs.
(4) The OED (　　) a very large dictionary of English and it (　　　　) the origins of words and their history.

GRAMMAR BANK

本文中から過去形の文を指摘して、その文の動詞を答えなさい。

(1) ＿＿＿＿＿＿ (2) ＿＿＿＿＿＿ (3) ＿＿＿＿＿＿ (4) ＿＿＿＿＿＿
(5) ＿＿＿＿＿＿

LESSON 6　　　　進行形

A. 現在進行形 (am [is, are]＋〜ing)

(1) **現在進行中の動作**を表す。
　1. Susan **is cooking** in the kitchen.
(2) **現在の反復的動作**を表す。always, constantly, all the time などの副詞（句）とともに用いられ、話し手のいらだち、驚き、非難などの気持ちを含むことが多い。
　2. The English language **is** *constantly* **changing**.
(3) **近い未来の予定**を表す。主として go, come, leave, arrive のような往来・発着を表す動詞が用いられる。
　3. I **am going** to Yokohama on business tomorrow.

B. 過去進行形 (was [were]＋〜ing)

1. He **was sleeping** when I entered the room.　〈過去の進行中の動作〉
2. She **was** always **asking** silly questions.　〈過去の反復的動作〉

C. 未来進行形 (will [shall] be＋〜ing)

1. It **will be snowing** tomorrow morning.　〈未来の進行中の動作〉
2. I **will be waiting** for the bus at five.　〈近い未来の予定〉

D. ふつう進行形をとらない動詞

(1) **知覚動詞**：see, hear, feel, smell, taste, *etc.*
　1. The rose **smells** sweet.
(2) **状態動詞**：be, have, know, love, think, belong, resemble, *etc.*
　2. He **resembles** his father.
　　[注] これらの動詞も意味によっては進行形にすることがある：
　　　This coat **has** no pockets. / He **is having** lunch with Brenda.

《チェックテスト6》

( )内の動詞を現在進行形か過去進行形に変えなさい。
1. He (take) a bath when the telephone rang.
2. We (leave) for Canada on Monday morning.
3. I (watch) the baseball game on TV last night.
4. Mary is busy now; she (clean) the living room.

EXERCISE 6

❶ 日本文の意味を表すように、次の各文の( )内に適語を補いなさい。

1. 私たちは土曜日にハイドパークへ行く予定です。
   We ( ) ( ) to Hyde Park on Saturday.
2. 私が起きた時、風が激しく吹いていた。
   The wind ( ) ( ) hard when I got up.
3. 彼女は娘を叱ってばかりいた。
   She ( ) ( ) her daughter all the time.
4. あなたが帰って来るころには雨が降っているでしょう。
   It ( ) ( ) ( ) when you come back.

❷ 次の各文の誤りを正しなさい。

1. I am knowing the way very well.

2. These oranges are tasting good.

3. She did her homework at that time.

4. Look! A black dog lies in the yard.

❸ 次の各文の意味を書きなさい。

1. I was taking a shower when the earthquake occurred.

2. He is always complaining about his noisy neighbor.

3. She will be singing a solo in the musical next season.

❹ 次の各文の( )内の語を並べ替えて正しい文にしなさい。

1. I (this / a / think / idea / is / good).

2. He (the / was / open / leaving / door / always).

3. They (be / in / next / traveling / Kyushu / week / will).

READING PASSAGE 6

The Storm

All day and all night it rained. "Can you hear that roar?" my brother asked me. "That's the roar of the water. The creek is running very high! I'd better go and take a look. I'm taking the flashlight. I won't be long." It was now two o'clock in the morning. There was no electricity. Outside, lightning lit up the sky. Water was gushing down the grassy pathway in front of the house.

An empty Styrofoam box outside was quickly filling with rain water. Inside, the candle in the kitchen was burning very low and the candle in the lounge room would not last the night. My mind began to race. "If our little stream in the valley is now a raging river, then this house might be in danger too!" I thought.

I was packing a little bag with some canned food and a change of clothes when my brother returned. "What are you doing, Joan?" he asked. I told him that (1)<u>I was getting ready to escape.</u> "Don't be silly!" he said. "This house will never flood. The fences are down and the cattle are out, but don't worry. (2)<u>Friends are coming tomorrow to help bring them back.</u>" I suggested that we go to higher ground. "Nope!" he said firmly. "The rain is starting to ease off already. (3)<u>Tomorrow, the sun will be shining again.</u>" Although I still felt nervous, I decided to go to bed.

Next morning, there was not a cloud in the clear blue sky. It was a beautiful day to start repairing fences.

24

NOTES

roar「とどろき、鳴り響く音」 **creek**「細流、川」 **run high**「水位が高くなる」 **I won't be long.**「長くはかからない、すぐに戻る」 **lightning**「稲妻」 **light up**「〜を明るく照らす」 **gush**「湧き出る」 **Styrofoam**「発泡スチロール」 **burn low**「火力が弱る、弱く光る」 **lounge room**「居間」 **last**「持ちこたえる」 **race**「(心が)はやる」 **raging**「荒れ狂う」 **be in danger**「危機にひんしている」 **pack A with B**「AにBを詰める」 **Don't be silly!**「バカなことを言うな」 **flood**「水浸しになる」 **higher ground**「高台」 **Nope!** = **No** **ease off**「和らぐ」

STORY BANK

本文の内容と合っているものにはT、間違っているものにはFを書き入れなさい。

(1) (　) It was raining very hard and it was two o'clock in the morning.
(2) (　) The author and her brother were riding in a boat on a raging river.
(3) (　) The author was getting ready to escape when her brother returned.
(4) (　) They were planning to repair fences the following day, but it was still raining.

CULTURAL BANK

英文を聞いて空所に適切な語を書き入れなさい。

(1) Lightning is a powerful flash of (　　　　) in the sky, usually followed by (　　　　).
(2) Thunder is the loud explosive (　　　　) that usually follows a flash of (　　　　).
(3) Styrofoam is a trademark of the Dow Chemical (　　　　) and the product is composed of (　　　　) percent air.
(4) "Hungry?"
  "(　　　　). I just (　　　　)."

GRAMMAR BANK

本文中の下線部(1)〜(3)の進行形の用法を、22ページの文法解説を参考に答えなさい。

(1) _____
(2) _____
(3) _____

LESSON 7 　　　完了形 (1)

A. 現在完了形(have [has]＋過去分詞) ― 過去の動作・状態が何らかの意味で現在につながっていることを示す。

(1) 現在までの動作の**完了**、その**結果**としての状態を表す。
   just, already, yet, recently などの副詞を伴うことが多い。「ちょうど[すでに]〜してしまった、など」「〜してしまって(今は)…だ」
   1. **Has** he **come** *yet*? ― No, he **hasn't come** *yet*.　　　〈完了〉
   2. I **have lost** my car key. (I don't have it now.)　　　〈結果〉

(2) 現在までの**経験**の有無を表す。ever, never, before, once, twice などの副詞を伴うことが多い。「〜したことがある[ない]」
   3. **Have** you *ever* **ridden** a roller coaster?
   4. I **have been** [《米》**gone**] to Fukuoka by bus.

(3) 現在までの**状態の継続**を表す。for …, since …, how long などの副詞句を伴うことが多い。「…の間[以来](ずっと)〜だ」
   5. I **have known** Mr. Rivers *for fifteen years*.
   6. He **has been** in the hospital *since last week*.

   [注]現在完了形は、yesterday, last week, two days ago のような明らかに過去を示す副詞(句)や疑問詞 when とともに用いることはできない：
   The game **started** *five minutes ago*. [正]
   The game **has started** *five minutes ago*. [誤]

B. 現在完了進行形 (have [has] been 〜ing) ― 現在までの動作の継続を表す。for…, since…, how long などの副詞句を伴うことが多い。「…の間[以来]〜している[してきた]」

   1. He **has been teaching** chemistry *for six years*.
   2. I'm sorry I'm late. **Have** you **been waiting** long?

《チェックテスト7》

( )内の動詞を現在完了形か現在完了進行形に変えなさい。
1. She (be) sick in bed since last Monday.
2. They (play) volleyball since morning.
3. I (listen) to the music for three hours.
4. He isn't at home now. He (go) to the library.

EXERCISE 7

◇①◇ 日本文の意味を表すように、次の各文の(　)内に適語を補いなさい。

1. あなたはタイへ行ったことがありますか。
   (　　　) you ever (　　　) to Thailand?
2. 私はまだ作文を書いていません。
   I (　　　) (　　　) my composition yet.
3. 昨夜から雪が降っています。
   It (　　　) (　　　) (　　　) since last night.

◇②◇ 次の各文の誤りを正しなさい。

1. When has the business seminar begun?

2. It has been very hot last summer.

3. We live in Seattle for nine years.

4. He is working in the bank since 1995.

◇③◇ 次の各文の意味を書きなさい。

1. I haven't heard from him since he went to England.

2. My brother has been absent from school for five days.

3. Ann has been taking fitness classes since last year.

4. I am not hungry because I have just finished my lunch.

◇④◇ 次の各文の(　)内の語を並べ替えて正しい文にしなさい。

1. I (such / never / a / seen / garden / have / pretty).

2. He (three / been / Greek / for / has / studying / years).

3. They (not / the / yet / have / computer / hacker / caught).

READING PASSAGE 7

Public Works for the State and for the Citizens

(1)<u>For many centuries, the pyramids have been a mystery</u>. Along with the Colosseum and other natural and man-made wonders, the Great Pyramid of Giza is one of the Seven Wonders of the World.

(2)<u>Many scholars from various fields have studied the pyramids for a long time</u>. There were historians, anthropologists, and even architects and engineers. They asked many questions such as: Who made the pyramids? How did they make them? Why did they make them?

For nearly 4,000 years, the Great Pyramid of Giza, also known as the Pyramid of Khufu, was the tallest man-made structure on earth. At the time of their construction, Egypt prospered. There are many theories on how they were built. One theory is that there was one long ramp outside that led up to the middle on one side. (3)<u>A French architect, Jean-Pierre Houdin, has published a new theory</u>. (4)<u>Houdin and his father, an engineer, have been working on this theory since 1999</u>. Houdin says that there was one low ramp outside, and a long spiral-like ramp inside.

Many pyramids are the tombs of important leaders. People thought that slaves built the pyramids under orders of the ruling pharaoh. Modern technology and intensive study have found that the pyramids were not built by slaves, but by volunteers and skilled workers. In other words, the pyramids were public works. The government also employed farmers to build the giant structures at times of the year when they couldn't work on their farms — that is, when the Nile River flooded in summer. Also, workers took time off for family trips, or to nurse injuries and hangovers.

NOTES

Colosseum「コロセウム」(円形競技場)　**the Great Pyramid of Giza**「ギザの大ピラミッド」　**the Seven Wonders of the World**「世界七不思議」　**anthropologist**「人類学者」　**engineer**「技師」　**Khufu**「クフ王」(紀元前26世紀、エジプト第4王朝の王)　**ramp**「傾斜路」　**lead > led**「通じる」　**on one side**「(ピラミッドの)一面に」　**Jean-Pierre Houdin**「ジャン・ピエール・ウーダン」　**work on~**「~を研究する、~に取り組む」　**spiral-like ramp**「らせん傾斜路」　**outside/inside**「(ピラミッドの)外部・内部に」　**pharaoh**「国王」　**intensive study**「徹底した研究」　**public works**「公共事業」　**that is**「すなわち」　**hangover**「二日酔い」

STORY BANK

本文の内容と合っているものにはT、間違っているものにはFを書き入れなさい。

(1) (　) The Colosseum is also one of the natural wonders of the world.
(2) (　) When Egypt prospered, Jean-Pierre Houdin published his theory on the construction of the pyramids.
(3) (　) People once thought that the Great Pyramid was built by slaves.
(4) (　) Now people consider the construction of pyramids as a kind of public works project.

CULTURAL BANK

英文を聞いて空所に適切な語を書き入れなさい。

(1) The Seven Wonders of the World are the most (　　　　) and impressive ancient (　　　　) made by ancient peoples.
(2) Anthropologists study the human (　　　　), including its beliefs, social (　　　　) and organization.
(3) Houdin's father (　　　　) (　　　　) developing the idea that the pyramids were constructed from inside.
(4) The Nile is the longest river in the world. People in Egypt and Sudan have (　　　　) (　　　　) the water for farming for centuries.

GRAMMAR BANK

本文中の下線部(1)~(4)の完了形の用法を、26ページの文法解説を参考に答えなさい。

(1) _____ (2) _____
(3) _____ (4) _____

LESSON 8　　　完了形(2)

◆ **A. 過去完了形(had+過去分詞)**—過去のある時までの完了・経験・継続を表す。時の基準点が現在から過去に変わるだけで、用法は現在完了形と同じ。

　(1) 完了：「(その時には)～してしまっていた」
　　　1. My father **had** *already* **left** home when I got up.
　(2) 経験：「(その時までに)～したことがあった[なかった]」
　　　2. I **had** *never* **learned** Korean before that time.
　(3) 状態の継続：「(その時まで)ずっと～だった」
　　　3. He said that he **had been** very busy *for three days*.

◆ **B. 過去完了進行形 (had been～ing)** — 過去のある時までの動作の継続を表す。「(その時まで[その時より前から])ずっと～していた」

　　1. I **had been studying** English *for an hour* when he came in.
　Cf. I **was studying** English when he came in.[「英語を勉強する」という私の動作と、「部屋に入ってくる」という彼の動作が同時に行われていた場合]

◆ **C. 未来完了形(will [shall] have+過去分詞)**— 未来のある時までの完了・経験・継続を表す。

　(1) 完了:「(その時には)～してしまっているだろう」
　　　1. He **will have gotten** well *by the end of this week*.
　(2) 経験：「(その時までに)～したことになる」
　　　2. I **will have been** to Italy *four times* if I go there again.
　(3) 継続：「(その時まで)ずっと～しているだろう」
　　　3. The baby **will have slept** *for five hours* by noon.

《チェックテスト8》

( )内の動詞を過去完了形か未来完了形に変えなさい
1. They (arrive) in Chicago by six this evening.
2. I (never see) Mr. Green before that time.
3. Next August we (live) here for twenty years.
4. I (already finish) my work when she came back.

EXERCISE 8

① 次の各文の( )内から適切なものを選びなさい。

1. I (read / had read) about India before I went there.
2. By next month we (have moved / will have moved) to Shizuoka.
3. On October 15 we (will be married / will have been married) for twenty years.
4. The truck (was running / had been running) for two hours before the engine broke down.

② 次の各文の誤りを正しなさい。

1. He has been ill for two weeks when I visited him.

2. She said that she was waiting for me for an hour.

3. I have bought a new digital camera by next Tuesday.

4. If I see that YouTube clip again, I will see it three times.

③ 次の各文の意味を書きなさい。

1. He had never learned French before he entered college.

2. By the end of this month, all the roses will have died.

3. Next month my father will have been dead for six years.

4. The plane had already taken off when we reached the airport.

④ 次の各文の( )内の語を並べ替えて正しい文にしなさい。

1. He (car / sold / will / old / have / his) by next month.

2. She (to / been / CD / had / a / listening) until that time.

3. I (from / had / back / just / shopping / come) when he came.

Riding an Old Steam Train

(1)<u>We had already climbed up into the last car of the old steam train</u> when the conductor called, "All aboard!" Penny, the eldest, led us to our seats. "Oh, isn't it all so wonderful!" she said, and sat down on one of the leather-covered seats. Her eyes sparkled as she looked at the old red velvet headrest. Each compartment in this car could seat six people. We were a group of five: my two sisters, our parents and me. It was so luxuriously decorated that we thought it must have been a first-class car.

(2)<u>We had been waiting for this day ever since the early summer</u>, when father had first talked about this steam train excursion. We all enjoyed looking at a pamphlet advertising the trip. (3)<u>We had never ridden in a steam train before that time</u>, but we had heard about it from Grandpa. He told us about how the steam trains needed to stop for water and coal, and how the passengers would get out for a cup of tea.

In particular, I was fascinated with the many old photographs that decorated the car. They were placed above the headrest, under the rack. Each old photo was in a shiny wooden frame. There was one photo of some important-looking people, perhaps taken on Opening Day. (4)<u>I had been looking at another photo</u> of young men cutting cane by hand when father said, "This train used to travel through a cane-growing area." Then we heard the whistle, and the train slowly pulled out of the station.

NOTES

climb up into~「～に乗り込む」　**the last car**「最後尾の車両」　**steam train**「蒸気機関車」　**"All aboard!"**「皆さんご乗車ください」（出発の合図）　**lead A to B**「AをBまで案内する」　**leather-covered**「革張りの」　**compartment**「客室」　**seat~**「～人分の座席を持つ」　**first-class car**「一等車」　**advertise~**「～を広告する」　**grandpa**「おじいちゃん」　**get out**「降りる」　**important-looking**「偉そうに見える」　**take~**「（写真）を撮る」　**Opening Day**「開通の日」　**cane**「サトウキビ」　**pull out of ~**「～から出て行く」

STORY BANK

本文の内容と合っているものにはT、間違っているものにはFを書き入れなさい。

(1) (　) They have just boarded the last steam train.
(2) (　) Their cabin might have been a first-class carriage before.
(3) (　) All the family was looking forward to this excursion.
(4) (　) The photographs in the carriage told the history of this steam train.

CULTURAL BANK

英文を聞いて空所に適切な語を書き入れなさい。

Thomas is a tank engine and displays the number one. It (1)(　　　) (　　　) blue with red lining. His friends include Edward, Henry, (2)(　　　), James and Percy. Thomas the Tank (3)(　　　) series is set on the Island of Sodor. It is a fictional island. The fictional island is in the Irish Sea, (4)(　　　) England (5) (　　　) the Isle of Man.

GRAMMAR BANK

本文中の下線部(1)～(4)の完了形の用法を、30ページの文法解説を参考に答えなさい。

(1) _____
(2) _____
(3) _____
(4) _____

LESSON 9　助動詞(1)

A. can の用法

(1) 能力：「〜(することが)できる」
 1. He **can** ride a horse. / He **can't** ride a horse.
   [注]未来形は will can とはならず、will be able to を用いる。
(2) 許可：「〜してもよい」
 2. **Can** (=**May**) I use this dictionary?
(3) 強い疑い：「いったい〜だろうか」、否定的推量：「〜のはずがない」
 3. How **can** she be so unkind?
 4. He **cannot** be an honest man.

B. may の用法

(1) 許可：「〜してもよい」、(否定文で)禁止：「〜してはいけない」
 1. **May** I go for a swim this afternoon?
   —Yes, you **may**. / No, you **may** [**must**] **not**.
   [注]may not は不許可を、must not は強い禁止を表す。
(2) 推量：「〜かもしれない」
 2. He **may** know the fact. / He **may not** know the fact.

C. must の用法

(1) 必要・義務：「〜しなければならない」
 1. **Must** I show it to him now?
   —Yes, you **must**. / No, you **don't have to** [**needn't**].
(2) 肯定的推量：「〜にちがいない」
 2. She **must** be angry with him.
   [注]過去形には had to を、未来形には will have to を用いる。

《チェックテスト9》

( )内に **can, may, must** から適語を補いなさい。
1. I think I (　　　) have a fever.
2. He (　　　) stand on his head.
3. (　　　) she really be his aunt?
4. All passengers (　　　) wear seat belts.

EXERCISE 9

⟨1⟩ 日本文の意味を表すように、次の各文の（ ）内に適語を補いなさい。

1. そのうわさは本当であるはずがない。
   The rumor ( ) ( ) true.
2. 彼は今、会社にいないかもしれない。
   He ( ) ( ) be in the office now.
3. 彼女は80歳を超えているにちがいない。
   She ( ) ( ) over eighty years old.
4. あなたは病院に行く必要はありません。
   You ( ) ( ) ( ) go to the hospital.

⟨2⟩ 次の各文の誤りを正しなさい。

1. She will can walk again before long.

2. Must I go so soon? — No, you must not.

3. You will must take an umbrella with you.

⟨3⟩ 次の各文の意味を書きなさい。

1. That cannot be Mrs. Smith; she is in London.

2. Can it be true that he was once in prison?

3. You must not show this memo to anyone else.

4. If you ask her again, she may change her mind.

⟨4⟩ 次の各文の（ ）内の語を並べ替えて正しい文にしなさい。

1. Can (here / some / I / for / stay / time)?

2. You (run / the / not / in / may / passageway).

3. We (to / early / morning / had / the / start / next).

READING PASSAGE 9

Farm Stays

Going overseas is a good way to learn about other cultures. You (1)<u>can</u> learn a foreign language as well. Some students take a break from their university studies to travel around Europe or Asia. Other students (2)<u>may</u> use their summer or winter holidays to take short trips overseas.

The style of travel and length of stay varies. Many people attend language schools, but you (3)<u>don't have to</u> go to special classes to pick up a language. Just by living with a family or a small group, you can learn a lot about a country. Some people like to do volunteer work at kindergartens or orphanages. If you can get a working holiday visa, you can work for wages and then use that money to tour around.

When Erika was in college, she decided to go to Holland. She stayed on a farm for three weeks. She looked after three little children while their parents painted the house. She also (4)<u>had to</u> help on the farm. Before returning to Japan, she spent two days touring around Amsterdam. She enjoyed the experience very much. Ten years later, she decided to go to Norway. She went with her young daughter. Again she went to work on a farm.

"When you go overseas, don't just stay in the cities. You really must go out into the countryside to learn more about the people and their culture," she says. In both countries, Erika used English on a daily basis, and also learned about farming, rural cuisine and many other things as well.

NOTES

Some ~. Other ~.「~する(学生)もいれば、~する(学生)もいる」　**take a break**「中断する」　**vary**「異なる」　**pick up~**「~を習得する」　**kindergarten**「幼稚園」　**orphanage**「児童養護施設」　**working holiday**「ワーキング・ホリデー」　**work for wages**「賃金を得て働く」　**tour around**「旅をして回る」　**Holland**「オランダ」　**look after~**「~の世話をする」　**Amsterdam**「アムステルダム」(オランダの首都)　**on a daily basis**「毎日」　**farming**「農業」　**rural cuisine**「田舎の料理」

STORY BANK

本文の内容と合っているものにはT、間違っているものにはFを書き入れなさい。

(1) (　　) If you go overseas you can learn not only a language but also about a culture.
(2) (　　) Attending language schools is not the only way to learn a foreign language.
(3) (　　) Erika went to work on a farm in Norway because she did not enjoy her stay in Holland.
(4) (　　) If you go overseas to learn a language, you should go out into the countryside because you can learn more than just the language.

CULTURAL BANK

CD 19

英文を聞いて空所に適切な語を書き入れなさい。

(1) If you (　　　　) have a working holiday visa, you (　　　　) work and study in a foreign country.
(2) Amsterdam is the capital (　　　　) of Holland, but the (　　　　) is based in the Hague.
(3) A gap (　　　　) is a year between leaving school and going to university. In the U.K., some young people use it as an opportunity to (　　　　), earn money or get working experience.
(4) The Normans are people from Normandy in northern (　　　　). They originally came from Norway and they later took (　　　　) of England in the 11th century.

GRAMMAR BANK

本文中の下線部(1)~(4)の助動詞の用法を、34ページの文法解説を参考に答えなさい。

(1) _____　(2) _____
(3) _____　(4) _____

LESSON 10　助動詞 (2)

A. would の用法

(1) 過去の習慣：「～したものだった」
    1. I **would** often go fishing in the river.

(2) 過去の拒絶：「どうしても～しなかった」
    2. He **would not** [**wouldn't**] listen to my advice.

(3) ていねいな表現：「～していただけませんか」
    3. **Would** you pass me the mustard?

B. should, ought to の用法

(1) 義務・当然：「～すべきである」
    1. Drivers **should** [**ought to**] obey the speed limit.

(2) 感情・判断・命令・決定・提案などの表現に続く **that** 節で
    2. It is natural [strange] that she **should** think so.
    3. He insisted [ordered] that I **should** go [《米》go] there alone.

C. used to の用法

(1) 過去の習慣：「～するのが常だった」
    1. She **used to** practice the piano every day.

(2) 過去の状態：「以前は～だった」
    2. There **used to** be a video rental shop here.

D. 「助動詞＋have＋過去分詞」の用法

1. He **may have forgotten** about the meeting.「～したかもしれない」
2. I **must have taken** the wrong road.「～したにちがいない」
3. The climber **cannot have lost** his way.「～したはずがない」
4. You **should** [**ought to**] **have come** earlier.「～すべきだったのに」

《チェックテスト10》

（　）内に would, should, used to から適語を補いなさい。

1. There (　　　) be a bookstore near here.
2. They (　　　) often talk about soccer.
3. It is important that everyone (　　　) attend.

EXERCISE 10

⟨①⟩ 日本文の意味を表すように、次の各文の( )内に適語を補いなさい。

1. 君たちは最善を尽くすべきだ。
   You (　　　) (　　　) do your best.
2. 彼はどうしても私の質問に答えなかった。
   He (　　　) (　　　) answer my question.
3. われわれは以前、同じ課で働いていた。
   We (　　　) (　　　) work in the same section.
4. 彼女がその就職面接に失敗したはずはない。
   She (　　　) (　　　) failed the job interview.

⟨②⟩ 次の各文の誤りを正しなさい。

1. You ought to tell me about it long ago.

2. He hasn't come yet. He may miss the train.

3. The teacher ordered that they would be silent.

⟨③⟩ 次の各文の意味を書きなさい。

1. It is a pity that he should have died so young.

2. Would you show me the way to the art gallery?

3. We would often go to karaoke when we were not busy.

4. He used to go out every night when he was a student.

⟨④⟩ 次の各文の( )内の語を並べ替えて正しい文にしなさい。

1. You (to / have / doctor / gone / the / should).

2. It is (so / she / strange / say / that / should).

3. He (his / busy / have / with / must / been / work).

Is Sunshine Really Bad for Us?

In 1981, Cancer Council Australia began a very successful campaign against skin cancer. The main character was a seagull. The seagull tells TV audiences to slip on a T-shirt, slop on sunscreen and slap on a hat. It also says that we should seek some shade, and slide on sunglasses when we are outside in the sun.

Australians love to be outdoors. Many schools don't even have a gym. On the other hand, a school with three or four sports grounds is not rare. Adults also enjoy the outdoors. Parks have picnic tables for families and groups. Many people like to go fishing on a lake or river. And everyone loves to spend time at the beach. But nearly everyone (1)<u>used to</u> go without any protection. They (2)<u>would</u> get sunburnt, but they (3)<u>wouldn't</u> worry very much. Then skin cancer became a big problem. In 2012, more than 2,000 people died of skin cancer in Australia.

But is sunshine really bad for us? What happens when we don't get enough sunshine? Actually, not enough sunshine is also a problem of modern society. Sunshine makes us strong. Sunshine makes us feel good. When we go out in the sunshine, our skin produces Vitamin D. Vitamin D is very important for our bodies. It helps make strong bones. It stops depression. It lowers high blood pressure. It helps us sleep well.

Without sunshine, our risk of getting heart disease or getting Alzheimer's increases. Doctors insist that especially young children (4)<u>should</u> go outside and play in the sunshine more.

NOTES

Cancer Council Australia「オーストラリアがん評議会」　　**skin cancer**「皮膚がん」
seagull「カモメ」　　**slip on~**「~をするっと着る」　　**slop on~**「~をぱっとかける」
sunscreen「日焼け止め(の薬)」　　**slap on~**「~をぽいとかぶる」　　**slide on sunglasses**「サングラスをすっとかける」　　**gym**「体育館」　　**picnic table**「ピクニック用食事テーブル」　　**protection**「保護」　　**sunburnt** = **sunburned**「赤く日に焼ける」
depression「憂うつ」　　**blood pressure**「血圧」　　**heart disease**「心臓病」
Alzheimer's (disease)「アルツハイマー(病)」

STORY BANK

本文の内容と合っているものにはT、間違っているものにはFを書き入れなさい。

(1) (　) A seagull began a successful campaign against skin cancer.
(2) (　) Australians like to go outside but they did not think about the risk of getting sunburn.
(3) (　) Sunshine makes us strong and feel good but sometimes may make us feel depressed.
(4) (　) Too much sunshine increases the risk of getting heart disease and Alzheimer's.

CULTURAL BANK

英文を聞いて空所に適切な語を書き入れなさい。

(1) Cancer is a diseased (　　　) in the body, which (　　　) cause death.
(2) Any particular type of (　　　) is named by a (　　　) of the alphabet.
(3) Alzheimer's is an illness that (　　　) and gradually (　　　) parts of the brain, especially in older people.
(4) In the U.S., the law says that the level of protection from sunburn (　　　) be indicated on the sunscreen product. You (　　　) see the numbers such as SPF30 or SPF50 on the bottle.

GRAMMAR BANK

本文中の下線部(1)~(4)の助動詞の用法を、38ページの文法解説を参考に説明しなさい。

(1) _____　(2) _____
(3) _____　(4) _____

LESSON 11 関係詞(1)

◆ **A. 関係代名詞** ― 代名詞と接続詞の2つの働きをする語。関係代名詞の導く節が修飾する名詞または代名詞を先行詞という。

 1. That is *the man*. **He** runs the bakery.
       who runs the bakery. 〈主格〉
 2. Show me *the clock*. You bought **it** last week.
       which you bought last week. 〈目的格〉

◆ **B. 関係代名詞の用法**

 (1) **who**：先行詞が人の場合に用いられる。
  1. A postal worker is *a person* **who** delivers letters.
  2. He has *a sister* **whose** name I can't remember.
  3. Dr. Brown is *a scholar* (**whom**) we all respect.
   ［注］①目的格の関係代名詞は、とくに《口語》では省略するのが普通である。
     ② whose は先行詞が物の場合にも用いられる：Use *a word* **whose**
      meaning is clear to you.

 (2) **which**：先行詞が物・動物の場合に用いられる。
  4. *The steak* (**which**) she cooked was very nice.
  5. He owns *the horse* **which** won the race.

 (3) **that**：先行詞が人・物のいずれの場合にも用いられるが、先行詞が形容詞の最上級や、all, the only, the same, the first, the very などの修飾語句を伴う場合は、とくに that が好んで用いられる。
  6. This is *the finest house* (**that**) I have ever seen.
  7. She was *the only girl* **that** was wearing earrings.
  8. He was *the first student* **that** raised his hand.
  9. You are *the very person* (**that**) I wanted to see.

《チェックテスト11》

次の各文の( )内に適切な関係代名詞を補いなさい。
1. The boy ( ) came to see me was Harry.
2. The house ( ) roof is green is mine.
3. These are photos (   ) show my family.
4. I bought the same dictionary ( ) you have.

EXERCISE 11

〈1〉次の2つの文を関係代名詞を用いて1文にしなさい。

1. The woman is Frank's aunt.　　She spoke first.

2. The road was very narrow.　　It led to his house.

3. I know a man.　　His son is now in Spain.

4. This is the dress.　　My mother made it for me.

〈2〉日本文の意味を表すように、次の各文の（ ）内に適語を補いなさい。

1. 人間は笑う唯一の動物である。
   Man is the (　　) animal (　　) laughs.
2. 表紙が茶色の本は私の本です。
   The book (　　) (　　) is brown is mine.
3. 彼は最初にエベレスト山に登頂した人です。
   He is the (　　) man (　　) climbed Mt. Everest.

〈3〉次の各文の意味を書きなさい。

1. Edward has a dog that barks loudly at everybody.

2. A child whose parents are dead is called an orphan.

3. This is the very skateboard I have long wanted to buy.

4. Dr. Yukawa is one of the greatest scientists that Japan has ever produced.

〈4〉次の各文の（ ）内の語を並べ替えて正しい文にしなさい。

1. Where (the / came / is / parcel / today / that)?

2. This (same / I / is / earring / lost / the / that).

3. I (man / speak / employed / Chinese / could / a / who).

READING PASSAGE 11

What's in a Name?

Have you ever thought about why the town you live in has that name? Many Japanese place names come from the geography of the land. Take, for example, the town of Shirakawa, (1)<u>which</u> got its name from the fast-flowing, white water of the river that flows by the town. That white water is the melting snow of Mt. Haku, a mountain (2)<u>that</u> has patches of white snow even in summer.

There are many towns in Australia (3)<u>which</u> keep the names the Aborigines used for those places. For example, Cooroy comes from the word for possum, and Maroochydore means "place of the black swan." Some towns were named after important people. Australia's largest city got its name from Lord Sydney, the man (4)<u>who</u> approved the first English township there in 1788.

American place names show how international the country is. Montana, for example, is Spanish for "mountain," and Vermont got its name from the French words for "green mountain." Many places in America got their names from the original hometown of the first English people or Europeans (5)<u>that</u> settled there. You can find Boston in Massachusetts and in Lincolnshire, England. New York is named after the English Duke of York, but the Dutch who lived there before the English used to call it New Amsterdam.

England was invaded many times during its long history. Each group of invaders brought their language with them. Cambridge is Old English, or Anglo-Saxon, and described the town around the bridge (6)<u>that</u> crossed the river Cam. However, Selby is from Danish, meaning "the town with the willow tree" and Bellister is from French, meaning "beautiful site."

NOTES

geography「地形」　fast-flowing「早く流れる」　melt「溶ける」　patch「まだら、部分」　Aborigine「アボリジニ」(オーストラリア先住民)　Cooroy「クーロイ」　Maroochydore「マルーチードール」(ともに、クイーンズランド州南東部のサンシャインコーストの町)　possum「フクロネズミ」　Lord Sydney「シドニー卿」(英国の政治家)　approve~「~を承認する」　township「町」　Lincolnshire, England「イングランドのリンカンシャー州」　Old English「古英語」(5~11世紀の英語)　Anglo-Saxon「アングロサクソン語」(現英国人の祖先の言語)　the river Cam「カム川」　Selby「セルビー」　Bellister「ベリスター」(ともに、イングランド北部のヨーク近郊の町)

STORY BANK

本文の内容と合っているものにはT、間違っているものにはFを書き入れなさい。

(1) (　) The town of Shirakawa is named after the geography of the land.
(2) (　) All of the place names in Australia came from either important English people or Aborigines.
(3) (　) Most of America's place names came from French.
(4) (　) The name of the town Cambridge means "a beautiful bridge."

CULTURAL BANK

CD 23

英文を聞いて空所に適切な語を書き入れなさい。

New England, (1)(　　　　) was the first place to be settled by the British, consists of (2)(　　　　) states: Maine, New Hampshire, Vermont, Massachusetts, Rhode Island and Connecticut. Boston, (3)(　　　　) is the most important city in New England and one of the oldest cities in the U.S., is a city in the state of Massachusetts. When people in the U.S. think of (4)(　　　　), they think of the neatly painted white wooden houses and brightly colored leaves (5)(　　　　) fall from the trees in fall.

GRAMMAR BANK

本文中の下線部(1)~(6)の関係代名詞の先行詞を答えなさい。

(1) _____　(2) _____
(3) _____　(4) _____
(5) _____　(6) _____

LESSON 12　　関係詞（2）

◇ **A. 関係代名詞と前置詞**―関係代名詞が前置詞の目的語になる場合、前置詞は関係代名詞の前に置くか、または関係代名詞の導く節の終わりに置く。
　　1. Is that the office **in which** [×that] you work?　　《文語》
　　2. Is that the office (**which**) you work **in**?　　《口語》

◇ **B. what の用法**―先行詞を含む関係代名詞で、「～するもの[こと]」という意味を表す。
　　1. **What** you need is more fresh fruit.
　　2. He is not **what** he was ten years ago.
　　3. Michael Jackson was **what we call** a superstar.「いわゆる」

◇ **C. 関係副詞の用法**―副詞と接続詞の2つの働きをする語で、where, when, why, how の4つがある。また、先行詞はしばしば省略される。
　　1. He walked to (*the place*) **where** I was standing.
　　2. It was *a time* **when** there were no computers.
　　3. That's (*the reason*) **why** she resigned.
　　4. This is **how** we wash our hands.[how は先行詞なしで用いる]

◇ **D. 限定用法と継続用法**―関係詞の導く節が先行詞の意味を限定するものを限定用法といい、先行詞の内容を補足説明するものを継続用法という。継続用法では、ふつう関係詞の前にコンマが置かれる。
　　1.　a. He has *two daughters* **who** became hairdressers.　　〈限定用法〉
　　　　b. He has *two daughters*, **who** (=and they) became hairdressers.
　　　　　　　　　　　　　　　　　　　　　　　　　　　　　　　〈継続用法〉
　　2.　a. This is *the hotel* **where** I stayed last summer.　　〈限定用法〉
　　　　b. I went to *Hiroshima*, **where** (=and there) I met my old friend.
　　　　　　　　　　　　　　　　　　　　　　　　　　　　　　　〈継続用法〉

《チェックテスト12》

次の各文の（　）内に適切な関係詞を補いなさい。
1. That is the house in (　　　) my uncle lives.
2. This is (　　　) he earned so much money.
3. (　　　) happened after that was interesting.
4. The reason (　　　) she hates him is not clear.

EXERCISE 12

<①> 日本文の意味を表すように、次の各文の( )内に適語を補いなさい。

1. 彼はあなたがいっしょに働いている人ですか。
   Is he the man (　　　) (　　　) you work?
2. 私が最も好きなのは読書です。
   (　　　) (　　　) (　　　) best is reading.
3. あれは私たちが泊まるホテルですか。
   Is that (　　　) (　　　) (　　　) we will stay?
4. このようなわけで、彼はオーディションに失敗したのです。
   (　　　) (　　　) (　　　) he failed the audition.

<②> 次の各組の文を、関係詞の用法に注意して和訳しなさい。

1. a. I bought some fresh eggs which had just come from the farm.
   b. He bought me a watch, which I don't like very much.
2. a. Winter is the season when we can enjoy skiing.
   b. Wait till next Friday, when I will pay you the money.
3. a. This is the place where the bus accident occurred.
   b. He then moved to New York, where he lived for six years.

<③> 次の各文の意味を書きなさい。

1. The office where he works is not far from here.

2. Do you know the reason why he quit his job?

3. I have two daughters, one of whom became a nurse.

4. She is the new manager of whom I spoke the other day.

<④> 次の各文の( )内の語を並べ替えて正しい文にしなさい。

1. He (a / what / call / fraud / we / is).

2. This (he / information / how / gathered / new / is).

3. That is (for / works / company / she / the / which).

You Are What You Eat

"You are (1)<u>what</u> you eat." This expression used to mean (2)<u>that</u> you should be careful about how much you eat. In other words, if you eat too much fatty food or sugar, you will gain weight and increase your risk of a heart attack.

Again, doctors are warning us, "You are what you eat." However, this time, they mean that our mood changes depending on what we eat. In other words, there are some foods (3)<u>that</u> make us happy or sad, active or sleepy.

Jetro Rafael from Manila, (4)<u>where</u> he owns a restaurant, tells his customers to wrap the ingredients on their plates in cabbage leaves. "Eating cabbage makes us happy," he says. Salmon is also on the menu, because it contains Vitamin B-12 and Omega-3 (5)<u>which</u> help fight depression. "And bananas are the happy fruit," he adds.

Experts say that fried foods like fried chicken and potato chips might taste good at the time (6)<u>when</u> you are eating them, but they will lead to depression. They also warn us (7)<u>that</u> alcohol and caffeine stop us from getting sleep, and getting not enough sleep leads to depression.

In order to get a good night's sleep, try eating some almonds or walnuts, or lettuce and tuna, suggests one dietician. A bowl of rice or some honey will also help you go to sleep, says another. One expert in sports nutrition says that if people want to have more energy, they should drink more water, or eat foods (8)<u>that</u> contain water, such as broccoli, carrots and watermelons.

NOTES

fatty「油っこい」　**heart attack**「心臓発作」　**mood**「心的状態、気分」　**wrap A in B**「AをBで包む」　**ingredient**「（料理の）材料」　**cabbage leaf**「キャベツの葉」　**Omega-3**「オメガ・スリー（脂肪酸）」（魚に含まれる不飽和脂肪酸）　**help (to) do**「～するのを助ける」　**happy fruit**「（食べると）幸せになる果物」　**fried**「油で揚げた」　**potato chip**「【英】フライドポテト」（【英】ポテトチップスはcrips）　**get a good night's sleep**「一晩ゆっくり眠る」　**walnut**「クルミ」　**dietician/dietitian**「栄養士」　**a bowl of rice**「茶碗1杯分のご飯・米」　**sports nutrition**「スポーツ栄養学」

STORY BANK

本文の内容と合っているものにはT、間違っているものにはFを書き入れなさい。

(1) (　) "You are what you eat" used to refer to the amount of food we should eat in order to lose weight.

(2) (　) "You are what you eat" now refers to foods affecting how we feel.

(3) (　) Cabbage, salmon and bananas are all what we call "happy food."

(4) (　) Fried chicken and potato chips taste good and they help us get a good night's sleep.

CULTURAL BANK

25

英文を聞いて空所に適切な語を書き入れなさい。

(1) Vitamin B-12, (　　　) is important for our body, is found in most animal (　　　), including fish, eggs and milk.

(2) Broccoli is a vegetable (　　　) young green (　　　) heads are edible.

(3) Deep-fried long strips of potato are called (　　　) fries in America and potato chips in (　　　).

(4) Thin slices of potato, (　　　) are sold in packets, (　　　) called potato chips in America and potato crisps in England.

GRAMMAR BANK

本文中の下線部(1)〜(8)を関係代名詞、関係副詞、その他の3つに分類し、番号で答えなさい。

1. 関係代名詞　_____　_____　_____　_____
2. 関係副詞　　_____　_____
3. その他　　　_____　_____

LESSON 13　　　　態（1）

◆ A. 受動態のつくり方

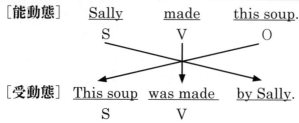

(a) 能動態の目的語（O）を主語（S）にする。
(b) 動詞（V）を「be＋過去分詞」の形に変える。
(c) 能動態の主語を「by＋(代)名詞」の形にして、文尾に置く。
(d) 動作主が一般の人々や不明の場合は、ふつう「by＋(代)名詞」は表されない：This bird **is called** a swan. / He **was killed** in the war.

◆ B. 基本的な構文の受動態

(1)「主語＋動詞＋目的語」の構文
　　1. a. Mr. Grant **wrote** this letter.（this letter＝目的語）
　　　 b. This letter **was written** by Mr. Grant.
(2)「主語＋動詞＋間接目的語＋直接目的語」の構文
　　2. a. He **gave** me this toy.（me＝間接目的語、this toy＝直接目的語）
　　　 b. I **was given** this toy by him.
　　　 c. This toy **was given** (to) me by him.
(3)「主語＋動詞＋目的語＋補語」の構文
　　3. a. The news **made** them happy.（them＝目的語、happy＝補語）
　　　 b. They **were made** happy by the news.
(4) 否定文・疑問文
　　4. This meat **was not cooked** by my mother.
　　5. **Was** this meat **cooked** by your mother?

《チェックテスト13》

次の各文を受動態に書き換えなさい。

1. My sister washed the dishes.
2. Miss Aoki teaches us history.
3. We found the cat dead on the road.
4. Did your father make the model car?

EXERCISE 13

① 次の各文を能動態に書き換えなさい。

1. Is he liked by every client?

2. Butter is not used in this cake.

3. English is spoken in Australia.

4. A long report was sent me by him.

5. She was made sad by the movie.

② 次の各組のbがaの受動態になるように、( )内に適語を補いなさい。

1. a. We call this flower a primrose.
   b. This flower (　　　) (　　　) a primrose.
2. a. Lucy made some cookies for us.
   b. Some cookies (　　　) (　　　) for us by Lucy.
3. a. We did not invite him to the dinner party.
   b. He (　　　) (　　　) (　　　) to the dinner party.

③ 次の各文の意味を書きなさい。

1. The telephone was invented by Bell in 1876.

2. She was killed instantly in the plane crash.

3. Hokkaido is visited by many foreign tourists.

④ 次の各文の( )内の語を並べ替えて正しい文にしなさい。

1. I (given / by / this / was / Marian / document).

2. Laser printers (that / sold / store / not / at / are).

3. A clean fork (waiter / to / the / me / was / by / brought).

A Car for the Blind?

A car for the blind? "Impossible!" you might say. Yet in 2010, researchers at Virginia Tech accomplished just that. The idea for a vehicle for the blind began in 2007, when the university entered a competition to build driverless vehicles. The competition was funded by the U.S. Defense Department.

Virginia Tech's vehicle had sensors to catch traffic and cameras to act as eyes. The technology is called "nonvisual interfaces." Later, they also developed a vibrating vest that told the blind driver to speed up or slow down. Other interfaces included special gloves that signaled when to turn right or left.

Experiments to make driverless cars, also called autonomous cars, began almost 100 years ago. Over the years, some companies have developed automatic cruise control technology and emergency stop technology, but driverless cars and cars for the blind were thought to be just a dream. In 2015, an autonomous vehicle traveled more than 5,000 kilometers across the U.S. from San Francisco to New York.

The car was fitted with radar, cameras and laser sensors. It was driven by drivers on only two short occasions: once in busy traffic and once during road works. One engineer explained that the car traveled smoothly along the highways, and the radar was not troubled by metal bridges. However, sometimes other drivers were made angry by the car's keeping exactly to the speed limit all the way.

These results seem very promising, but several obstacles remain. These include driving in rain or snow, and the need for advances in computer technology.

NOTES

the blind「盲人」　**Virginia Tech**「バージニア工科大学」　**enter~**「~に参加する」　**driverless**「運転手のいない」　**fund~**「~に資金を供給する」　**the U.S. Defense Department**「米国国防総省」(通称ペンタゴン)　**traffic**「往来、交通量」　**nonvisual interface**「視覚にたよらない装置」　**vibrate**「震動する」　**glove**「手袋」　**when to turn right or left**「右か左にいつ曲がるか」　**autonomous**「自律（運転）の」　**automatic cruise control**「自動速度制御装置」　**emergency stop**「非常停止」　**fit A with B**「AにBを取り付ける」　**road works**「道路工事」　**all the way**「ずっと」　**promising**「将来有望な」

STORY BANK

本文の内容と合っているものにはT、間違っているものにはFを書き入れなさい。

(1) (　) The idea for a vehicle for the blind was developed when Virginia Tech entered a competition.
(2) (　) Nonvisual interfaces include things such as sensors, cameras, a vibrating vest and special gloves.
(3) (　) Along the way to developing autonomous vehicles, companies have developed automatic cruise control and emergency stop technologies.
(4) (　) In 2015, a driverless vehicle traveled all the way across the U.S.

CULTURAL BANK

 27

英文を聞いて空所に適切な語を書き入れなさい。

(1) A car (　　　) (　　　) running at a steady speed by cruise control technology.
(2) Cities (　　　) usually (　　　) by highways. Freeways are high-speed roads within a city.
(3) San Francisco is (　　　) for being a very beautiful city and it is (　　　) on hills overlooking a bay facing the Pacific Ocean.
(4) A pentagon is a five-sided shape, a hexagon (　　　), a heptagon seven and an (　　　) eight.

GRAMMAR BANK

本文中から受動態の文を指摘し、例のように主語とbe動詞+過去分詞を書き出しなさい。

(1) The competition was funded　　(2) _____
(3) _____
(4) _____　(5) _____
(6) _____　(7) _____

LESSON 14　　　態 (2)

◆A. 注意すべき受動態

1. a. *Who* **baked** the bread?　　　　　　　　〈Who で始まる疑問文〉
   b. *By whom* **was** the bread **baked**?《文語》
   c. *Who* **was** the bread **baked** *by*?《口語》［実際には、あまり用いられない］
2. a. We **can see** the city from here.　　　　　〈助動詞を伴う場合〉
   b. The city **can be seen** from here.
3. a. He **has planted** the daffodil bulbs.　　　　〈完了形〉
   b. The daffodil bulbs **have been planted** by him.
4. a. The birds **are building** a nest.　　　　　　〈進行形〉
   b. A nest **is being built** by the birds.
5. a. The doctor **took care of** the patient.　　　〈群動詞〉
   b. The patient **was taken care of** by the doctor.
6. a. **They [People] say that** he is a great movie director.
   　　　　　　　　　　　　　　　　　　　　　〈「～だそうだ」の表現〉
   b. **It is said that** he is a great movie director.
   c. He **is said to** be a great movie director.

◆B. by 以外の前置詞を用いる受動態 ― 感情や心理状態を表す受動態の後には、by でなく at, in, to, with などの前置詞が用いられる。

1. We **were surprised at** his decision.「～に驚く」
2. He **is known to** all the villagers.「～に知られている」
3. **Are** you **pleased with** the result?「～に満足している」
4. Your hands **are covered with** flour!「～で覆われている」
5. I **am interested in** classical music.「～に興味がある」

《チェックテスト14》

次の各文を受動態に書き換えなさい。
1. Who made this Japanese doll?
2. You will find the task difficult.
3. Mr. Hill has written those poems.
4. My daughter looked after the baby.
5. They say that he is a famous movie star.

EXERCISE 14

① 次の各文の態を変えなさい。

1. Who painted this picture?

2. An ambulance must be called at once.

3. We have often discussed the problem.

4. A foreigner spoke to me this morning.

5. A new hotel is being built near the station.

② 次の各組の b が a の受動態になるように、(　)内に適語を補いなさい。

1. a. We can see a full moon this evening.
   b. A full moon (　　　) (　　　) (　　　) this evening.
2. a. The sight surprised them very much.
   b. They (　　　) very much (　　　) (　　　) the sight.
3. a. The whole audience laughed at the comedian.
   b. The comedian (　　　) (　　　) (　　　) by the whole audience.

③ 次の各文の意味を書きなさい。

1. My friend Albert is interested in tropical fish.

2. It is sometimes said that money brings happiness.

3. A lecture on the universe is being given by Dr. Hawking.

④ 次の各文の(　)内の語を並べ替えて正しい文にしなさい。

1. Our dog (a / run / truck / over / was / by).

2. He (to / in / known / the / everybody / is / town).

3. The manager (sales / plan / is / with / new / pleased / the).

Talking Drums

Music plays an important part in the lives of many people. In Zimbabwe, there is a well-known proverb: If you can walk, you can dance. If you can talk, you can sing.

Since time began, music has been influenced by language, and language in turn has been influenced by music. Also, the type of music played in each region of the world is influenced by the way people move between countries. For example, American blues and jazz have roots in African music. The blues is said to have started as African American work songs. The rhythm of southern gospel music is often compared to the rhythm of traditional African songs.

Along with rhythm, instruments can also be taken to other regions where they are changed to fit the music style of the new region. The Chinese 18-stringed *guzheng* is an example of this. In Japan, it became a 13-stringed *koto*. In Vietnam, it became the short *dan tranh*. However, not all instruments follow this pattern.

Similarities can also be seen between the African talking drum and the Japanese *kotsuzumi* drum. Both instruments are shaped like an hourglass with cords running between each end. The player puts pressure on the cords to change the pitch. While the African talking drum imitates spoken words and phrases, and was often used to send messages between villages, the *kotsuzumi* drums are usually only played at Noh drama or Kabuki performances. Although they may look similar, they have different backgrounds. It is said that the Japanese drum came from India via China while talking drums are from western Africa.

NOTES

play a part「役を務める」　**lives**「生活」(lifeの複数形)　**since time began**「有史以来」　**in turn**「代わって」　**move**「移動・移住する」　**African American**「アフリカ系アメリカ人の」　**along with~**「~に加えて」　**take A to B**「AをBに持って行く」　**fit~**「~に適応させる」　**18-stringed**「18弦ある」　**guzheng**「グーチェン、古箏」　**dan tranh**「ダンチャイン、弾箏」　**talking drum**「トーキングドラム」(遠距離通信用のドラム)　**hourglass**「砂時計」　**cord**「ひも(縦調べ、横調べ)」　**run**「延び(てい)る」　**put pressure**「(握って)圧力をかける、張力を加減する」　**via~**「~を経て」

STORY BANK

本文の内容と合っているものにはT、間違っているものにはFを書き入れなさい。

(1) (　) Language and music have influenced each other for a long time.
(2) (　) We do not know the roots of American blues and jazz at all.
(3) (　) Musical instruments hardly change their shapes, even when they are used in different regions.
(4) (　) The African talking drum and the Japanese *kotsuzumi* drum have different backgrounds but are similar in shape.

CULTURAL BANK

英文を聞いて空所に適切な語を書き入れなさい。

(1) Zimbabwe was formerly known as Rhodesia and was (　　　) (　　　) the British from 1889.
(2) African Americans (　　　) originally (　　　) to the U.S. as slaves in the 18th and 19th centuries.
(3) Vietnam (　　　) (　　　) by France, as part of French Indochina, from the mid-19th century.
(4) Gospel music, which is usually (　　　) by African Americans, is a style of religious music with songs which are (　　　) strong and loud.

GRAMMAR BANK

本文中から受動態の文を探し、例のように、その動詞の原形を書き出しなさい(重複可)。

(1) <u>influence</u>　(2) _____　(3) _____　(4) _____
(5) _____　(6) _____　(7) _____　(8) _____
(9) _____　(10) _____　(11) _____　(12) _____

LESSON 15   不定詞（1）

「to+動詞の原形」の形で、名詞・形容詞・副詞の働きをする。

◆ A. 名詞用法

(1)「〜すること」という意味を表し、文中で主語・補語・目的語として用いられる。
1. **To walk** with him was a pleasure. 〈主語〉
   ［注］*It* was a pleasure **to walk** with him. となるのがふつう。
2. My aim in life is **to become** a novelist. 〈補語〉
3. Where do you plan **to spend** your vacation? 〈目的語〉

(2) how, what などの疑問詞と結びついて、「〜のしかた」「何を〜したらよいか」などの意味を表す。
4. He taught me **how to ski**.
5. Tell me **what to do** next.

◆ B. 形容詞用法 ── 不定詞が名詞・代名詞を後ろから修飾する用法。

1. He has no *time* **to read**.
2. This is a good *way* **to make** friends.
3. Please give me *something* **to eat**.

◆ C. 副詞用法 ── 文中で副詞として用いられ、いろいろな意味を表す。

1. We eat **to live**, not live **to eat**.「〜するために」 〈目的〉
2. I was surprised **to hear** the news.「〜して」 〈原因〉
3. You are careless **to make** such a mistake.「〜するとは」 〈理由〉
4. This room is difficult **to heat**.「〜するのに」 〈限定〉
5. He grew up **to be** a great artist.「…して〜になる」 〈結果〉

《チェックテスト15》

次の各文の（ ）内に適語を補いなさい。
1. (   ) is unwise to waste time.
2. There was no bench to sit (   ).
3. I have a large family (   ) support
4. Do you know (   ) to spell the word?

EXERCISE 15

⟨①⟩ 次の各文の下線部と同じ用法の不定詞を含む文を、下から選びなさい。

1. He had no friends to help him.　　　　　　　(　　)
2. My plan is to go abroad to study.　　　　　　(　　)
3. This manual is hard to understand.　　　　　 (　　)
4. I don't want to discuss it now.　　　　　　　 (　　)
5. He taught me how to turn the DVD player on.　(　　)

   (a) These vegetables are easy to grow.
   (b) He is not a man to tell a lie.
   (c) I asked him where to change trains.
   (d) Her dream is to be a fashion designer.
   (e) I promised to return the book the next day.

⟨②⟩ 日本文の意味を表すように、次の各文の(　)内に適語を補いなさい。

1. 彼は最初にウイルスを発見した人だった。
   He was the first man (　　　) (　　　　) the virus.
2. 彼女は成長して、すてきなお嬢さんになった。
   She grew up (　　　) (　　　　) a fine young lady.
3. そのリンゴを切るためのナイフをお持ちですか。
   Do you have a knife (　　　) cut the apple (　　　　)?

⟨③⟩ 次の各文の意味を書きなさい。

1. A good restaurant is hard to find in this town.

2. How to live is the most important thing in life.

3. You are silly to spend so much money on clothes.

⟨④⟩ 次の各文の(　)内の語を並べ替えて正しい文にしなさい。

1. We (hoping / again / visit / are / England / to).

2. She (home / change / clothes / to / went / her).

3. I was (bad / hear / very / to / the / sorry / news.)

READING PASSAGE 15

The Future for Farmers

Farming is an important primary industry. Economies depend on it. Many people think it is a good, healthy way (1)<u>to make a living</u>. Three farmers, each from a different country, were asked what problems they thought farmers might face in the future.

Peter, from Oregon, U.S.A. predicts problems dealing with water. Every year in spring, Peter has to pay $1,600 for a permit to take water from a nearby stream for his wheat farm. He expects the cost of the permit to rise in the future. "If the price of the water permit rises, some people may decide (2)<u>to quit farming</u>," he says.

Bill, a pineapple farmer in the eastern state of Queensland, Australia, believes that big corporate farms will continue to buy up small farms, and then only grow specific high-earning crops, like corn for biofuel. "If big farms produce crops (3)<u>to make fuel</u> and not food, Australia will lose its agricultural diversity," he says.

Tsuneo, like Peter and Bill, is in his seventies, and has seen many changes over the past sixty years. He is now a major landowner in Hokkaido. His farm continues to produce enough potatoes to supply a large supermarket chain. His biggest concern at the moment is the long-term influence of the Trans-Pacific Partnership on farms like his. "I'm lucky that my granddaughter and her husband are helping me now. But we need more young men and women (4)<u>to come up with new ideas</u>," he says. Then he smiled and added, "You know, you need farmers every day, three times a day!"

NOTES

primary industry「第一次産業」　**make a living**「生計を立てる」　**face~**「~に直面する」　**deal with~**「~を扱う」　**permit**「(利用)許可」　**wheat farm**「小麦農場」　**some people ~**＝ there are some people~「~という人もいる」　**big corporate farm**「巨大な法人組織の農場(企業)」　**buy up**「買い占める」　**high-earning crops**「収益性の高い農作物」　**biofuel**「バイオ燃料」　**diversity**「多様性」　**long-term**「長期の」　**Trans-Pacific Partnership ＝ TPP**「環太平連携協定」　**come up with new idea**「新しい考えを思い付く」　**three times a day**「1日に3回」

STORY BANK

本文の内容と合っているものにはT、間違っているものにはFを書き入れなさい。

(1) (　) Economies do not depend on primary industries any more.

(2) (　) Peter, from Oregon, may decide to quit farming if he does not get enough rain for his crops.

(3) (　) Bill, from Queensland, wants big corporate farms to buy his farm.

(4) (　) Tsuneo, Peter and Bill are old farmers and all of them are anxious about the future of agriculture.

CULTURAL BANK

英文を聞いて空所に適切な語を書き入れなさい。

(1) Primary (　　　) includes agriculture, forestry, (　　　) and mining.

(2) To be in the secondary industry is (　　　) produce manufactured goods and to work in the tertiary industry is to (　　　) services.

(3) A biofuel is a fuel that is derived from biological materials such as (　　　) and (　　　).

(4) There are (　　　) countries participating in the (　　　) negotiations.

GRAMMAR BANK

本文中の下線部(1)と同じ不定詞の用法を(2)~(4)から選び記号で答えなさい。

(1) _____

LESSON 16　不定詞(2)

A. 注意すべき不定詞の用法

1. He *seems* **to be** idle. (=It *seems* that he **is** idle.)
2. He *seems* **to have been** idle. (=It *seems* that he **was** idle.)
3. I was old **enough to** work and earn money.「～するほど」
4. This tea is **too** hot **to** drink.「あまり…なので～できない」

B. 〈It is ～ for [of]…to do〉の構文

1. It is quite strange *for us* **to meet** here.「…が～するのはまったく不思議だ」
2. It was careless *of you* **to forget** your passport.「～するなんて…は不注意だった」

C. 原形不定詞(to のつかない不定詞)の用法

(1) 知覚動詞 (see, hear, feel, *etc*.)+目的語+原形不定詞
　1. We *saw* him **enter** the coffee house.
　2. I *heard* the clock **strike** seven.

(2) 使役動詞 (make, let, have, *etc*.)+目的語+原形不定詞
　3. Mama *made* me **cook** dinner.「(強制的に)～させる」
　4. I *had* her **clear** the table.「～させる、してもらう」
　[注]1,2,3 の文を受動態にすると to が必要になる：He *was seen* **to enter** the coffee house. / I *was made* **to cook** dinner by mama.

D. 原形不定詞を含む慣用表現

1. We'*d better* **go** before it gets dark.「～するほうがよい」
2. I *would rather* **die** than **steal**.「BよりもむしろAしたい」

《チェックテスト16》

次の各文の(　)内に適語を補いなさい。
1. He was made (　　) repeat the story.
2. It was very good (　　) you to come.
3. I would (　　) stay home than go out.
4. This problem is (　　) difficult to solve.

EXERCISE 16

① 次の各文の( )から適切なものを選びなさい。
1. Mark always makes me (laugh / to laugh).
2. It's stupid (for / of) you to smoke so much.
3. I think you had better (go / to go) by bus.
4. He was seen (come / to come) out of the room.
5. She seems (to be / to have been) ill for a long time.

② 日本文の意味を表すように、次の各文の( )内に適語を補いなさい。
1. ポールは有能な医者らしい。
   Paul seems ( ) ( ) an able doctor.
2. 私は1時間以上待たされた。
   I was made ( ) ( ) for over an hour.
3. 彼はあまり太っているので、自分の靴のひもが結べない。
   He is ( ) fat ( ) tie his own shoes.
4. 雄太にその箱を台所へ運ばせよう。
   I'll ( ) Yuta ( ) the box to the kitchen.

③ 次の各文の意味を書きなさい。
1. I heard someone call out for help in the dark.

2. She wouldn't let her daughter go out at night.

3. It is natural for parents to love their children.

4. This hotel is large enough to hold about 1,000 people.

④ 次の各文の( )内の語を並べ替えて正しい文にしなさい。
1. She (her / sweep / had / floor / son / the).

2. We (last / felt / house / night / shake / the).

3. I (a / across / saw / river / swim / the / dog).

The Extraordinary Steve Jobs

Steve Jobs was a brilliant man. It is not an exaggeration for us to say that Steve Jobs changed the world. He was an inventor and a businessman. He was the co-founder and CEO of Apple Inc. There he helped develop and sell the first Macintosh computer, the iMac, iPod, iPhone and iPad. As the head of NeXT Inc., he developed the first "workstations" for use in universities.

Jobs was a very creative man. He entered Reed College in Oregon in 1972, but wanted more freedom. He dropped out after six months. The college, however, let him attend classes that interested him. A calligraphy course that he took there was his favorite. Thanks to that calligraphy course, the Mac computer has many creative fonts and typefaces.

But (1)<u>Jobs also seems to have been an eccentric man</u>. He would rather walk around barefoot than wear socks and shoes. One day, Jobs went barefoot to ask a certain rich man for money for a special project. (2)<u>The rich man</u> got very angry and <u>made him leave the office</u> immediately. He said that Jobs was too bad-mannered and dirty to lend money to.

Jobs was also a great fan of Japan and Japanese things. He wore clothes designed by Issey Miyake and he often visited Kyoto to enjoy the food and culture there. He even sent the chef of the company cafeteria to Japan to learn how to make soba noodles. Actually, Jobs was very concerned about his health, both physically and spiritually. He followed Japanese Zen Buddhism.

NOTES

brilliant「異彩を放つ」　**co-founder**「共同創設者」　**CEO** = **Chief Executive Officer**「最高経営責任者」　**Inc.**「法人（組織の）」　**help (to) do**「〜するのを助ける」　**NeXT**「ネクスト」（ワークステーション名）　**workstation**「中央のシステムに連結した端末装置」　**Reed College**「リードカレッジ」　**drop out**「中退する」　**calligraphy**「カリグラフィー」（手書き装飾文字、その手法）　**thanks to~**「〜のおかげで」　**creative**「個性的な」　**font**「活字」　**typeface**「書体」　**eccentric**「風変わりな」　**barefoot**「素足で」　**bad-mannered**「行儀の悪い」　**dirty**「汚い、汚れている」　**Issey Miyake**「三宅一生」　**company cafeteria**「社員食堂」

STORY BANK

本文の内容と合っているものにはT、間違っているものにはFを書き入れなさい。

(1) (　　) Steve Jobs was too brilliant to change the world.

(2) (　　) Mac computers have many creative fonts and typefaces.

(3) (　　) The rich man was happy to meet Steve Jobs because he came barefoot.

(4) (　　) Jobs liked Japanese food so he invited a famous soba chef to the company cafeteria.

CULTURAL BANK

英文を聞いて空所に適切な語を書き入れなさい。

(1) Apple is a U.S. computer company (　　　　) best known product is the Macintosh personal (　　　　).

(2) NeXT developed and manufactured a series of computer (　　　　) intended for the higher education and business (　　　　).

(3) NeXT was founded in (　　　　) by Apple Computer co-founder Steve Jobs, after he and a few of his (　　　　) were forced out of Apple.

(4) Issey Miyake is a world famous Japanese (　　　　) who was (　　　　) in Hiroshima in 1938.

GRAMMAR BANK

下線(1)をItで始まる文に、(2)を受動態に書き換えなさい。

(1) _____

(2) The rich man made him leave the office.

_____

LESSON 17　　　分詞 (1)

分詞には**現在分詞**と**過去分詞**の2種があり、いずれも名詞を修飾する**限定用法**と、補語の働きをする**叙述用法**とがある。

A. 分詞の限定用法 ― 分詞が単独で名詞を修飾する場合は名詞の前に置かれるが、分詞が他の語句を伴う場合は名詞の後に置かれることが多い。

1. Don't wake up the **sleeping** *baby*. 〈単独で名詞を修飾する場合〉
2. The *boy* **feeding** the birds is Ted. 〈分詞が目的語を伴う場合〉
3. She stepped on the **broken** *cup*. 〈単独で名詞を修飾する場合〉
4. This is a *fruit* **called** "avocado." 〈分詞が補語を伴う場合〉

B. 分詞の叙述用法

(1) **主格補語として**：主語について何事かを述べる。
　1. The puppy came **running** to its mother.
　2. He seemed **shocked** by her sudden death.

(2) **目的格補語として**：目的語について何事かを述べる。
　3. I'm very sorry to keep you **waiting**.
　4. Can you make yourself **understood** in Spanish?
　　「自分の考えを人に分からせる」

(3) **知覚動詞+目的語+分詞**
　5. I *saw* him **running** across the street. 〈動作の途中〉
　　Cf. I *saw* him **run** across the street. 〈動作の始めから終わりまで〉
　6. Have you ever *heard* Danish **spoken**?

(4) **have [get]+目的語+過去分詞**
　7. I'll *have* [*get*] the chair **mended**.「〜してもらう」 〈使役〉
　8. I *had* my wallet **stolen** in the train.「〜される」 〈被害〉

《チェックテスト17》

次の各文の(　)内の動詞を適切な形に変えなさい。
1. My daughter came home (cry) bitterly.
2. Our teacher gave us a (write) test.
3. This is a telescope (make) in Germany.
4. I caught him (listen) outside the door.

EXERCISE 17

⟨1⟩ 次の各文の(　)内に、下記の語群から適語を選び、必要に応じて形を変えて入れなさい。

1. I have my hair (　　　) every four weeks.
2. Don't use this word in (　　　) English.
3. He rushed out of the (　　　) building.
4. This is a poem (　　　) by a famous poet.
5. I caught him (　　　) money from my purse.
6. The birds (　　　) in the air are sparrows.

[burn / cut / fly / speak / take / write]

⟨2⟩ 次の各文の誤りを正しなさい。

1. Suddenly I heard my name calling.

2. I had a new house design by the architect.

3. He was lying on the bed read a magazine.

⟨3⟩ 次の各文の意味を書きなさい。

1. I had my hat blown off by the strong wind.

2. He seemed satisfied with his small income.

3. She noticed a green sedan following her car.

4. The lion sleeping in the cage came from Africa.

⟨4⟩ 次の各文の(　)内の語を並べ替えて正しい文にしなさい。

1. We (in / him / park / saw / jogging / the).

2. He (the / there / at / stood / children / looking).

3. I have (sung / French / never / this / in / heard / song).

READING PASSAGE 17

A Cool Memory

I remember the day very clearly. It was very hot. The tour bus picked us up at our hotel, and took us to a lovely place (1)called the Summer Palace. It is really an Imperial Garden with a large man-made lake, a man-made hill, and some interesting buildings. It lies in the north-western part of Beijing.

Our first stop was a long corridor running along the edge of the lake. For over 700 meters, we enjoyed viewing paintings of old folktales and legends of brave warriors. As we walked along the covered path, our guide told us that many emperors and empresses, princes and princesses had also walked here. We enjoyed the beautiful scenery and the cool breeze coming off the lake.

After a lunch of special court food, we boarded a red and yellow ferry. The 40-minute boat ride was very pleasant. It was interesting to see this side of that huge city. Willow trees shaded the canal. It was very cool. On the bank of the canal, (2)a friendly-looking man stood beside his bicycle and watched us pass. Another man was sleeping under one of the willows. Young children (3)wearing colorful clothes waved from arched bridges. The hustle and bustle of city life was forgotten.

At last we arrived at the Beijing Zoo. Our first stop? Panda House, of course. We had hoped to see some pandas playing. But it was, after all, a hot day. We only saw some pandas (4)sleeping. They were lying with their heads on their paws, and they seemed uninterested in all the people coming to see them.

NOTES

pick~ up「～を迎えに来る」　**the Summer Palace**「頤和園（いわえん）」　**Imperial Garden**「皇帝の庭園」　**man-made**「人工の」　**run**「延びる、広がる」　**folktale**「民話」　**covered path**「屋根付きの通路」　**off~**「～の沖に・から」　**court food**「宮廷料理」　**red and yellow**「赤と黄色に塗られた」　**willow tree**「柳の木」　**shade~**「～を陰にする」　**bank**「土手」　**friendly-looking**「親切そうな」　**pass**「通過する」　**arched**「弓形の」　**hustle and bustle**「押し合いへし合い」　**lie**「横たわる」　**with~**「～したまま」　**paw**「足」

STORY BANK

本文の内容と合っているものにはT、間違っているものにはFを書き入れなさい。

(1) (　　) There is a man-made lake and a man-made hill in the Summer Palace.
(2) (　　) They met emperors, empresses, princes and princesses when they were walking along the covered path.
(3) (　　) They boarded a ferry and then they ate a special lunch.
(4) (　　) The author saw pandas at the Beijing Zoo, but they were only sleeping.

CULTURAL BANK

英文を聞いて空所に適切な語を書き入れなさい。

(1) In (　　　　) 1998, UNESCO included the Summer Palace on its (　　　　) Heritage List.
(2) A ferryboat goes across a (　　　　) or any other especially narrow stretch of water, (　　　　) people and things.
(3) Beijing, (　　　　) Peking in English before, is the (　　　　) city of the People's Republic of China.
(4) The giant panda is a large animal from China that has (　　　　) and (　　　　) fur.

GRAMMAR BANK

本文中の下線部(1)～(4)の分詞の用法を、66ページの文法解説を参考に答えなさい。

(1) _____　(2) _____
(3) _____　(4) _____

LESSON 18   分詞(2)

A. 分詞構文 ― 分詞に導かれる句が文全体を修飾して、さまざまな意味を表すことがある。

(1) 時：when, while, after で書き換えられるもの。
　1. **Coming** to the bridge (=*When I came* to the bridge), I met Steve.

(2) 理由：as, because で書き換えられるもの。
　2. **Feeling** cold (=*As he felt* cold), he turned on the gas heater.

(3) 条件：if, unless で書き換えられるもの。
　3. **Turning** left (=*If you turn* left), you will see the building.

(4) 付帯状況：主に and で書き換えられるもの。
　4. We started at six, **arriving** there (=*and arrived* there) at ten.

　　［注］ 分詞の表す「時」が述語動詞の表す「時」よりも前の場合は、完了形の分詞構文(having+過去分詞)を用いる：**Having failed** (=*After I had failed*) several times, I succeeded.)

B. 独立分詞構文 ― 分詞の意味上の主語が文の主語と異なる場合は、意味上の主語を分詞の前に置く。

1. The day **being** fine, we went for a drive.
   (=*Because the day was* fine, we went for a drive.)
   ただし、次のような慣用表現では、分詞の意味上の主語が文の主語と異なっていても、その意味上の主語を省くことができる。
2. **Frankly speaking**, I don't agree with your idea.「率直に言えば」
3. **Generally speaking**, the presentation was good.「一般的に言えば」
4. **Talking** of illness, I hear Bob has lung cancer.「〜と言えば」
5. **Judging from [by]** his words, his work is going well.
   「〜から判断すると」

《チェックテスト18》

次の各文を(　)内の接続詞を用いて書き換えなさい。
1. Looking up at the sky, I saw a rainbow. (when)
2. It being warm, he took off his coat. (because)
3. Waving her hands, she said good-bye to us. (and)
4. Walking faster, you will catch up with her. (if)

EXERCISE 18

① 次の各文を分詞構文を用いて書き換えなさい。

1. She said thank you to us and went away.

2. As I had a bad headache, I went to bed early.

3. If you cross the bridge, you will see the harbor.

4. When I was weeding the garden, I was stung by a bee.

② 日本文の意味を表すように、次の各文の（　）内に適語を補いなさい。

1. 日曜日なので、その店は休みだった。
   (　　　) (　　　) Sunday, the store was closed.
2. 仕事を終えてから、私は散歩に出かけた。
   (　　　　) (　　　　　) my work, I went out for a walk.
3. 野球と言えば、あなたは中日ファンですか。
   (　　　　) (　　　) baseball, are you a Dragons fan?

③ 次の各文の意味を書きなさい。

1. Walking along the beach, I met a friend of mine.

2. Not knowing anyone in town, I felt lonesome.

3. Turning right, you will find the bank on the left.

4. Strictly speaking, this sentence is not grammatical.

④ 次の各文の（　）内の語を並べ替えて正しい文にしなさい。

1. (rained / night / it / all / having), the road was muddy.

2. He was reading, (wife / him / dress / sewing / beside / his / her).

3. Judging from his last letter, (is / a / time / he / having / wonderful).

Holmes? Watson?

Arthur Conan Doyle published his first Sherlock Holmes story in 1887. (1)<u>Appearing at first in literary magazines</u>, the stories were later arranged into anthologies, made into stage plays and movies, and adapted into easy-to-read books for EFL learners. The stories have also been translated into over 60 languages.

(2)<u>Being so popular,</u> the Sherlock Holmes stories have also been imitated by several amateur and professional writers. There are now nearly 2,000 pastiches, including some written by Doyle's son, Adrian Conan Doyle. In fact, some of the pastiches are so well written that even the Doyle Estate introduces them on its website.

Hugh Ashton is one such pastiche writer. Judging from the style of the stories in *Tales from the Deed Box of John H. Watson, MD*, it seems like one of the famous Arthur Conan Doyle books. But, (3)<u>looking at the cover</u>, you will see that it is not an original. Ashton remembers that he was talking with friends about the Sherlock Holmes stories at a dinner party in January 2012. The next day, he wrote his first Holmes story.

Ashton says he grew up with a complete set of Sherlock Holmes books, a gift from his grandmother for his 11th birthday. He quickly adds that research and life's experiences have helped him, too. For example, Ashton used his knowledge of the *Mikasa* to help him write *The Giant Rat of Sumatra*. So far, he has written 24 shorter adventures and two novels, nearly equaling half of Doyle's total Sherlock Holmes output.

NOTES

Arthur Conan Doyle「アーサー・コナン・ドイル」(1859~1930)　**Sherlock Homes**「シャーロック・ホームズ」　**literary magazine**「小説誌」　**arrange~**「~をまとめる」　**anthology**「選集本」　**stage play**「舞台劇」　**adapt~**「~を書き換える」　**easy-to-read**「読みやすい」　**EFL**「外国語としての英語」　**pastiche**「模倣作品」　**estate**「財団」　**Hugh Ashton**「ヒュー・アシュトン」（鎌倉在住の英国人小説家）　**deed box**「保管用書類・証書箱」　**John H. Watson**「ジョン・ワトソン」（ホームズの友人）　**MD** = **Doctor of Medicine**「医学博士」　**research**「研究」　**the Mikasa**「戦艦三笠」　***The Giant Rat of Sumatra***『スマトラの大鼠』　**equal~**「~に等しい」

STORY BANK

本文の内容と合っているものにはT、間違っているものにはFを書き入れなさい。

(1) (　) Conan Doyle wrote Sherlock Holmes stories for stage plays and movies.

(2) (　) Doyle's son introduces Sherlock Holmes stories by other authors on the website.

(3) (　) Hugh Ashton wrote some stories that people might think were original stories by Doyle.

(4) (　) Hugh Ashton read the Sherlock Holmes series when he was young.

CULTURAL BANK

英文を聞いて空所に適切な語を書き入れなさい。

(1) The detective Sherlock Holmes was a fictional (　　　　) (　　　　) by Conan Doyle.

(2) Doyle wrote about (　　　　) stories but there are many other Sherlock Homes stories which were not (　　　　) by Doyle himself.

(3) Adrian Conan Doyle was the youngest son of Doyle and (　　　　) the Sir Arthur Conan Doyle Foundation in Switzerland in (　　　　).

(4) EFL, which stands for English as a (　　　　) Language, is the use or study of English by speakers of different (　　　　) languages.

GRAMMAR BANK

本文中の下線部を接続詞を含む文に書き換えなさい。

(1) _____

(2) _____

(3) _____

LESSON 19　　　　　動名詞（1）

◆A. 動名詞の用法 ―「動詞の原形+ing」の形を持ち、名詞の働きをする。

1. **Flying** a kite is a lot of fun.　　　　　　　　　　　〈主語〉
2. My job is **driving** a tour bus.　　　　　　　　　　〈補語〉
3. She loves **singing** Irish folk songs.　　　　　　　〈目的語〉
4. He is good at **playing** the guitar.　　　　　　　〈前置詞の目的語〉

◆B. 動名詞と不定詞

(1) 動名詞と不定詞のどちらも目的語にとる動詞

　(a) 意味が同じもの：begin, start, continue, intend, attempt, *etc.*

　　1. The train began **speeding** [**to speed**] up.
　　2. It started **raining** [**to rain**] in the evening.

　(b) 意味が異なるもの：like, forget, remember, try, *etc.*

　　3. a. I remember **sending** the bill.「〜した覚えがある」
　　　　【bill：請求書】
　　　b. Remember **to send** the bill.「忘れずに〜する」
　　4. a. Jim tried **eating** sashimi, and he liked it.「〜してみる」
　　　b. Jim tried **to eat** sashimi, but he couldn't.「〜しようとする」

(2) 動名詞のみを目的語にとる動詞［群動詞］：avoid, enjoy, finish, mind, stop, give up, put off, *etc.*

　6. I really enjoy **being** with him.
　7. He gave up **smoking** five years ago.

(3) 不定詞のみを目的語にとる動詞：want, hope, desire, expect, plan, decide, promise, *etc.*

　8. I expect **to be** back on Friday.
　9. Do you want **to travel** abroad?

《チェックテスト19》

> 次の各文の（　）内の動詞を適切な形に変えなさい。
> 1. They decided (sell) the house.
> 2. I am not very fond of (dance).
> 3. We enjoyed (walk) in the park.
> 4. She promised (call) me every week.

EXERCISE 19

① 次の各文の下線部が動名詞であるものを選び、その用法を指摘しなさい。
1. You must avoid <u>eating</u> fatty food. (　　　　　)
2. <u>Rising</u> from his chair, he made a bow. (　　　　　)
3. My hobby is <u>collecting</u> alpine plants. (　　　　　)
4. Don't be afraid of <u>asking</u> for help. (　　　　　)
5. The girl <u>riding</u> a bicycle is my sister. (　　　　　)

② 次の各文を、動名詞と不定詞の用法に注意して和訳しなさい。
1. a. He suddenly stopped talking.
   b. He stopped to consult a map.
2. a. I remember giving him the keys.
   b. Remember to give him the keys.
3. a. I'll never forget reading the novel.
   b. Don't forget to bring the textbook.
4. a. He tried moving the heavy stone.
   b. He tried to move the heavy stone, but he couldn't.

③ 次の各文の意味を書きなさい。
1. He put off submitting the paper for a few days.

2. She tried dieting, but it had no effect on her.

3. Andy continued working part-time until August.

4. I enjoyed talking with him about a trip to Australia.

④ 次の各文の(　)内の語を並べ替えて正しい文にしなさい。
1. Don't (to / night / me / forget / tomorrow / phone).

2. How long (stay / you / to / Tokyo / intend / in / do)?

3. You (for / give / a company / such / up / should / working).

Aussie English

Making friends with people from other countries is great fun. But newcomers to Australia often have trouble with Australian English. Australians have a marked accent, and (1)<u>understanding</u> "Aussie slang" can be difficult sometimes.

Some typical Aussie words are actually old British English words. The word "tucker" is a good example of this. The noun "tucker" means "food" and comes from an early 19th century British English slang verb "to tuck (into)" meaning "to consume food or drink." Australians have taken the word and expanded its meaning, so we now have a "tucker box" which is a lunch box, and a "tuck shop" which is the school kiosk. But, beware. To be "tuckered out" refers to being exhausted after (2)<u>doing</u> some hard work, and is not connected to food at all.

Some Australian slang is difficult to understand because it uses (3)<u>rhyming</u>. Take "take a Captain Cook" for example. Captain Cook mapped Australia's eastern coast and his name rhymes with "look." Therefore the person who uses this phrase wants the listener to look at something. Also if you tell your friend that you are "on my Pat Malone," it is the same as being alone.

Perhaps, one thing Aussie English is famous for is (4)<u>using</u> diminutives. That is, the average Australian uses a lot of words that are shortened and then given an –o or –ie at the end. Therefore, "afternoon" is shortened to "arvo", and "Christmas" is cut down to "Chrissie." "Sunglasses" become "sunnies" and "servos" are "service stations."

NOTES

newcomer「新来者」　**have trouble with~**「～に手を焼く」　**marked**「著しい」　**Aussie**＝**Australian**「オーストラリアの」　**noun**「名詞」　**come from~**「～に由来する」　**verb**「動詞」　**consume~**「～を食べ尽くす、飲み尽くす」　**take~**「～を取り入れる」　**tuck shop/school kiosk**「学校の売店」　**exhausted**「疲れ切った」　**rhyme**「韻を踏む」　**take a Captain Cook**＝**take a look at**「見て!」　**map~**「～を測量・調査する」　**on my Pat Malone**＝**all alone**「独りぼっち」　**diminutive**「縮小語・指小接尾辞」（小ささを意味する接辞の付いた語、あるいは親愛の情を示す接辞）　**shorten~**「～を短くする」　**service station**「ガソリンスタンド」

STORY BANK

本文の内容と合っているものにはT、間違っているものにはFを書き入れなさい。

(1) (　　) Some Australian English expressions are different from the original British English both in their meanings and pronunciations.

(2) (　　) The words "tucker," "tuck into" and "tuckered out" all mean the same thing.

(3) (　　) The words "Cook" and "look" rhyme, but "Malone" and "alone" do not.

(4) (　　) Australian people like to cut down words and put -o or -ie at the end of them.

CULTURAL BANK

英文を聞いて空所に適切な語を書き入れなさい。

(1) Australian English began after the (　　　　　) of the colony of New South Wales in 1788 and was recognized as (　　　　　) different from British English by 1820.

(2) Slang is often used among particular groups of (　　　　　), but it is not used in serious speech or (　　　　　).

(3) The (　　　　　) of British English is called Received Pronunciation and is used as a model for (　　　　　) English to foreign learners.

(4) Captain Cook discovered several islands in the Pacific Ocean, (　　　　　) Hawaii, where he was (　　　　　).

GRAMMAR BANK

本文中の下線部(1)～(4)の動名詞の用法を、74ページの文法解説Aを参考に答えなさい。

(1) _____ (2) _____
(3) _____ (4) _____

LESSON 20　　動名詞（2）

◆ A. 動名詞の意味上の主語
(1) 文の主語と一致している場合、一般の人々 (we, they など)の場合などは、これを明示しない。
1. He is proud of (*his*) **being** a lawyer.　　　　〈文の主語と一致〉
2. (*Our*) **Walking** is good for our health.　　　　〈一般の人々〉

(2) 文の主語と異なっている場合には、(代)名詞の所有格または目的格を動名詞の前に置く。口語では、(代)名詞の目的格を用いる。
3. I am sure of *my son('s)* **coming** home safe.
4. I can't understand *your* [*you*] **divorcing** your wife.

◆ B. 完了形の動名詞（having＋過去分詞）
述語動詞よりも以前の「時」を明示したいときに用いる。
1. He denied **having** stolen the money.
(=He denied that he *had stolen* the money.)

◆ C. 形容詞的に用いられた動名詞（アクセントの位置に注意）
1. a **sléeping** bag「寝袋」/ a **sléeping** car「寝台車」　　〈動名詞〉
　Cf. a **sléeping** báby [cát]「眠っている赤ちゃん[ネコ]」　〈現在分詞〉

◆ D. 動名詞を含む慣用表現
1. *It is no use* **trying** to persuade him.「～してもむだだ」
2. I don't *feel like* **eating** now.「～したい気がする」
3. We just *couldn't help* **laughing**.「～せずにはいられない」
4. *There is no* **denying** the historical fact.「～できない」
5. *On* **arriving** in Kyoto, I telephoned my wife.「～するとすぐに」

《チェックテスト20》

次の各文を動名詞を用いて書き換えなさい。
1. Henry is ashamed that he is unemployed.
2. I am sure you will pass the examination.
3. There is no hope that he will get a job.
4. He regretted that he had lost his umbrella.

EXERCISE 20

〈1〉次の各文中の動名詞の意味上の主語を指摘しなさい。

1. Reading in bed is bad for your eyes.　　　　　（　　　　　）
2. My lifework is building a nursery school.　　　　　（　　　　　）
3. He is proud of having a luxurious mansion.　　　　　（　　　　　）
4. I am ashamed of my brother being a computer addict.　（　　　　　）

〈2〉次の各組の文がほぼ同じ意味になるように、（　）内に適語を補いなさい。

1. a. It is useless to worry about the past.
   b. It is (　　　) use (　　　　) about the past.
2. a. I have no wish to study tonight.
   b. I don't feel (　　　) (　　　　) tonight.
3. a. It is impossible to know what he will say.
   b. There is (　　　) (　　　　) what he will say.
4. a. She regretted that she had refused his offer.
   b. She regretted (　　　　) (　　　　) his offer.

〈3〉次の各文の意味を書きなさい。

1. I remember my father being very strict with us.

2. She couldn't help feeling sorry for the child.

3. I am sure of our team winning the football game.

4. He always carries a walking stick when he goes out.

5. On graduating from college, she went over to the United States.

〈4〉次の各文の（　）内の語を並べ替えて正しい文にしなさい。

1. He (his / afraid / job / of / is / losing).

2. I (you / don't / my / like / using / PC).

3. We (car / not / in / sleeping / should / the / smoke).

READING PASSAGE 20

Garfield

Garfield is a very intelligent talking cat. He "speaks" to his owner through speech bubbles in comics in your local newspaper. People can't help laughing at the things Garfield says and does.

Garfield was created by Jim Davis in 1978. Before (1)<u>creating</u> Garfield, Davis made a comic strip with a gnat as the main character. Editors liked his drawings, but the story wasn't popular. Davis needed to find a new character. Then he realized that cats didn't appear much in comic strips. Also, having grown up on a farm with 25 cats, he knew he could draw them well. So the character of Garfield was born.

The comic strip "Garfield" quickly became popular. It is now the most widely sold comic strip in the world. It is translated into more than 40 languages and appears in over 2,570 newspapers worldwide. On weekdays, Garfield appears in three-panel comics strips. On the weekends the stories are about seven or eight panels long. Garfield has starred in animated movies and programs for TV. He has a musical CD on sale as well.

Davis says, however, that his winning four Emmy awards has changed his way of writing the comic strip. Davis now wants to promote education. Garfield is still a lazy cat that loves (2)<u>eating</u> and watching TV, but he also likes reading. Garfield's image has been used on mobile libraries since 1994. In TV and magazine commercials, Garfield tells kids that (3) <u>reading</u> is like food for the brain, and sleeping at least nine hours a night makes you bright and alert. A free Professor Garfield internet site has educational games for children.

NOTES

Garfield「ガーフィールド」（コミックの主人公のネコの名前）　**speech bubble**「（漫画の）吹き出し」　**local**「地元の」　**comic strip**「（新聞の）連載漫画」　**gnat**「ブヨ」　**drawing**「デッサン、絵のタッチ」　**over~**「〜以上の」　**three-panel**「3コマの」　**star**「主役を演じる」　**on sale**「販売中の」　**Emmy awards**「エミー賞」　**promote~**「〜を促進する」　**mobile library**「移動図書館」　**kid**「子ども」　**a night**「一晩につき」　**alert**「機敏な」

STORY BANK

本文の内容と合っているものにはT、間違っているものにはFを書き入れなさい。

(1) (　　) Garfield is a real-life, very intelligent cat.
(2) (　　) "Garfield" was Jim Davis's first comic strip and the story wasn't very popular.
(3) (　　) Now we can enjoy "Garfield" everyday in the newspapers.
(4) (　　) Davis uses the image of Garfield to promote reading.

CULTURAL BANK

英文を聞いて空所に適切な語を書き入れなさい。

(1) Garfield was born in the kitchen of an (　　　　) restaurant and loves (　　　　) lasagna and pizza.
(2) An Emmy award is a (　　　　) given each year for special achievements in (　　　　).
(3) A mobile library or bookmobile is a (　　　　) that is kept in a (　　　　) and driven from place to place.
(4) Most (　　　　) newspapers have four to six (　　　　) pages full of comic strips such as "Peanuts," "Blondie" and "Garfield."

GRAMMAR BANK

本文中の下線部(1)〜(3)の動名詞の意味上の主語を答えなさい。

(1) _____　(2) _____　(3) _____

LESSON 21　　　　形容詞・副詞

A. 形容詞の用法
(1) **限定用法**：(代)名詞の前に置かれてそれを修飾するが、形容詞が他の語句を従えたり、-thing で終る代名詞を修飾する場合は後置される。
  1. He was wearing a **blue** *jumper*.
  2. She sat with her *eyes* **full** of tears.
  3. There is *something* **wrong** with my car.

(2) **叙述用法**：文中で主格補語・目的格補語として用いられる。
  4. It seems **impossible** to me.　　　　　　　　　　　〈主格補語〉
  5. I found the bed **comfortable**.　　　　　　　　　　〈目的格補語〉

(3) **限定用法と叙述用法で意味が異なるもの**
  6. a. The **present** governor is Mr. Winters.「現在の」
     b. The governor was **present** at the ceremony.「出席して」
  7. a. The **late** Mr. Jones was my close friend.「故〜」
     b. Mr. Jones was **late** for the last train.「〜に遅れて」

B. 副詞の用法 ── 副詞はふつう動詞・形容詞・他の副詞を修飾するが、副詞句・副詞節あるいは文全体を修飾することもある。

  1. "I'm sorry," he *said* **quietly**.　　　　　　　　　　〈動詞を修飾〉
  2. He is **very** *fond* of Italian food.　　　　　　　　〈形容詞を修飾〉
  3. Mike speaks Russian **quite** *well*.　　　　　　　　〈他の副詞を修飾〉
  4. They came here **exactly** *at ten o'clock*.　　　　〈副詞句を修飾〉
  5. She looks happy **only** *when she is* with you.　〈副詞節を修飾〉
  6. **Naturally** we are very disappointed.「当然」　　〈文全体を修飾〉
     (=It is natural that we are very disappointed.)
  Cf. Relax and *behave* **naturally**.「自然に」　　　　〈動詞を修飾〉

《チェックテスト21》

次の各文の後ろの(　)内の語を最も適切な位置に入れなさい。
1. You will find his advice. (helpful)
2. He was at the farewell party. (present)
3. Do you have anything to drink? (cold)
4. That tall gentleman is Mr. Yamamoto. (old)

EXERCISE 21

⟨1⟩ 次の各文の（　）内に、下記の語群から適語を選んで補いなさい。
1. The ship came (　　　) into the harbor.
2. It was (　　　) dark when I woke up.
3. The train got in at (　　　) ten o'clock.
4. (　　　) she knows nothing about it.
5. He is nearly (　　　) at home on Sundays.
6. A man is happy (　　　) when he is healthy.

[always / exactly / only / quite / slowly / strangely]

⟨2⟩ 日本文の意味を表すように、次の各文の（　）内に適語を補いなさい。
1. グレイスはとても悲しそうに見えた。
   Grace (　　　) very (　　　).
2. その箱はからであることが分かった。
   I (　　　) the box (　　　).
3. 現市長は私のおじです。
   The (　　　) (　　　) is my uncle.

⟨3⟩ 次の各文の意味を書きなさい。
1. The late Mr. Taylor was a famous violinist.

2. In the kitchen there was a large wooden table.

3. I ate curry and rice simply because I liked it.

4. Is there anything interesting in today's paper?

⟨4⟩ 次の各文の（　）内の語を並べ替えて正しい文にしなさい。
1. He (not / the opening / was / present / ceremony / at).

2. She (play / well / flute / can / quite / the).

3. I (full / him / book / sent / of / a / pictures).

Climbing

(1)<u>Proudly</u>, Toby stood at the top of Mount Kilimanjaro. In the photo he took to show his family back in the States, he was wearing the same red and brown sweater that his grandfather wore some fifty years before. Grandfather attempted to climb Mt. Everest. Will Toby climb Mt. Everest next? "Oh, no," he said. "I climbed Kilimanjaro because my Dad grew up in Kenya. I had always wanted to see the place. But one mountain is enough for me."

Mountain climbing is the pastime of many youths. When Yoshio was in his mid-twenties, he spent (2)<u>nearly</u> every summer weekend in the Japan Alps, climbing such mountains as Mt. Ontake, Mt. Yari and Mt. Hotaka, all over 3,000 meters high. But for Yoshio it was just a fad. When he got married, he stopped climbing just as easily as he had started.

For others, the thrill of reaching the summit of that first peak (3)<u>never</u> fades. They continue to climb time and time again. Lewis is a fit 55-year-old who climbs Mt. Fuji four or five times a year. Because he loves climbing (4)<u>so</u> much, he now guides small groups up the mountain. He wants them to experience the hardship of the climb, as well as the thrill of completing the feat. He also tells visitors that Mt. Fuji is a sacred mountain. He hopes that it will make them care more about the environment.

There are some people who see mountains as the ultimate challenge. At the age of 80, Yuichiro Miura made his third successful ascent of the world's highest mountain. He then become the oldest man ever to climb Mt. Everest.

NOTES

back「~に残っている」　**the States**「アメリカ合衆国」　**red and brown**「赤と茶のシマ模様の」　**some**「およそ」　**pastime**「娯楽」　**all**「どれもみな、すべて」　**over~**「~以上の」　**fad**「一時的な流行」　**others**「他の人々」　**summit**「頂上」　**that first peak**「(登った)最初のあの峰」(頂上を含む広い部分)　**time and time again**「再三再四」　**a fit 55-year-old**「55歳の健康な人」　**a year**「1年につき」　**hardship**「苦難」　**feat**「(登頂した)すばらしい行為」　**sacred**「神聖な」　**ultimate challenge**「究極の挑戦」　**ascent**「登頂」

STORY BANK

本文の内容と合っているものにはT、間違っているものにはFを書き入れなさい。

(1) (　) Toby's father grew up in Kenya and the family still lives in Africa now.
(2) (　) Yoshio gave up climbing mountains after he got married.
(3) (　) Lewis's job is guiding small groups up mountains in Japan.
(4) (　) Yuichiro Miura climbed the world's highest mountain three times.

CULTURAL BANK

英文を聞いて空所に適切な語を書き入れなさい。

(1) Kilimanjaro, a mountain in Tanzania, is the (　　　) mountain in Africa at (　　　) meters above sea level.
(2) Until it became an (　　　) country in 1963, Kenya was a member of the (　　　) Commonwealth.
(3) The origin of the name Fuji is (　　　). The name may have come from "(　　　)" (not + die) or "without equal" (not + two).
(4) Mt. Everest, which is in the Himalayas, is the highest mountain in the world and was (　　　) climbed in 1953 by Sir Edmund Hillary from New Zealand.

GRAMMAR BANK

本文中の下線部(1)~(4)の副詞の用法を、82ページの文法解説Bを参考に答えなさい。

(1) _____　(2) _____　(3) _____　(4) _____

LESSON 22　　　　比　較（1）

◆ A. 基本的な比較表現

(1) 原級によるもの
　1. Becky is *as* **old** *as* Peggy.「…と同じくらい～」
　2. Becky is *not as* [*so*] **old** *as* Fiona.「…ほど～でない」

(2) 比較級によるもの
　3. I like summer **better** *than* winter.「…より～」
　4. He is **more diligent** *than* I [me].［me がふつう］
　[注]　superior, inferior, senior, junior, prefer などを用いた比較表現
　　　では、than でなく to を伴う：He is two years **senior** [**junior**] *to* me. /
　　　My sister **prefers** cats *to* dogs.

(3) 最上級によるもの
　5. She is **the youngest** *of* the three.
　6. The Volga is **the longest** river *in* Europe.
　[注]　比較級を強める副詞には much, far, even などが、最上級を強める副詞
　　　句には by far がある：This is *much* [*far*] **better** than that. / She is
　　　by far **the best** ballet dancer.

◆ B. 比較構文の転換

1. a. John cannot ski *as* [*so*] **well** *as* Dick.
   b. Dick can ski **better** *than* John.
2. a. No other metal is *as* [*so*] **precious** *as* gold.
   b. Gold is **more precious** *than* any other metal.
   c. Gold is **the most precious** *of* all metals.
3. a. Nothing is *as* [*so*] **important** *as* time.
   b. Nothing is **more important** *than* time.
   c. Time is **the most important** thing (of all).

《チェックテスト22》

次の各文の（　）内に適語を補いなさい。
1. He prefers watching tennis (　　　　) playing.
2. A cheetah runs (the) fastest of (　　　　) wildcats.
3. This suit is (　　　　) more expensive than that one.

EXERCISE 22

①　次の各文の(　)内の語を、必要に応じて適切な形に変えなさい。
1. She can sing (well) than her sister.　　　　　(　　　　　)
2. We are even (busy) than yesterday.　　　　　(　　　　　)
3. Mont Blanc is (high) mountain in Europe.　　(　　　　　)
4. This box is not as (heavy) as that one.　　　　(　　　　　)
5. Henry drives (carefully) than anyone else.　　(　　　　　)

②　次の各組の文がほぼ同じ意味になるように、(　)内に適語を補いなさい。
1. a. She is three years older than Betty.
   b. She is three years (　　　　) (　　) Betty.
2. a. Matt is more handsome than Fred.
   b. Fred is (　　) as handsome (　　) Matt.
3. a. Friendship is the most precious of all things.
   b. (　　　　) is more precious (　　　　) friendship.
4. a. A giraffe is the tallest of all animals.
   b. A giraffe is taller than (　　) (　　　　) animal.

③　次の各文の意味を書きなさい。
1. No other state in the U.S.A. is as big as Alaska.

2. They have by far the largest house in the village.

3. He is clearly superior to all the other candidates.

4. The test was much more difficult than I had expected.

④　次の各文の(　)内の語を並べ替えて正しい文にしなさい。
1. He (it / than / knows / even / me / better).

2. She (junior / eight / Gloria / is / years / to).

3. This cloth (in / that / is / quality / to / one / inferior).

Lost in Translation

We depend on translation more than we realize. For example, newspaper reporters use translators and interpreters to get information for the articles they write about. (1)<u>Nothing is better than getting information directly from the people involved</u>, but reporters don't always speak the language of the country they are working in. That is why they use interpreters a lot. Translators also work on novels, movies, recipes, user manuals and research papers.

Perhaps, (2)<u>poetry is the most difficult form of literature to translate</u> because it sometimes has words with double meanings. Perhaps the poet chooses a word because of its sound or because it rhymes with another. These things are difficult to translate. If the translator adds everything, the translation will be become much longer than the original.

The term "lost in translation" is used when we think an idea or a concept has not been translated fully from one language to the other. What many people don't realize is that the "loss" is not always an accident. Sometimes translators prefer to "lose" words or phrases, or perhaps even paragraphs. Perhaps the content is socially inappropriate. Perhaps the content or place names are not known to foreign readers. Take Yasunari Kawabata's *The Izu Dancer*, for example. The Japanese version opens with a string of place names. However, the English version only says, "… three nights at hot springs near the center of the peninsula."

"A translated novel should be as good a book to read as the original one," says one translator. "Sometimes I will also change the grammar and sentence structure to make the translation better."

NOTES

article「記事」　involved「関係している」　not always「いつも~とは限らない」　work「勤めている」　a lot「ずいぶん」　work on~「~に取り組む」　user manual「取り扱い説明書」　research paper「研究・調査報告書」　rhyme with~「~と韻をふむ」　another = another word　lose in translation「翻訳して原作の趣を失う」　loss「翻訳しないこと」　socially inappropriate「社会的に不適切な」　a string of~「一連の~」　peninsula「半島」　good a book to read「そん色なく読める本」

STORY BANK

本文の内容と合っているものにはT、間違っているものにはFを書き入れなさい。

(1) (　) Interpreters work on written papers, and translators transfer spoken content to another language.

(2) (　) It is hard to translate poetry because the translators can not understand the meanings of the words.

(3) (　) Translators sometimes prefer not to translate some words, phrases or even sentences that were in the original.

(4) (　) There are some translators who even change the sentence structure of a book to make it better.

CULTURAL BANK

45

英文を聞いて空所に適切な語を書き入れなさい。

The Izu Dancer is a (1)(　　　) story written in 1926 and was (2)(　　　) translated into English by Edward Seidensticker in 1955. Seidensticker is said to be (3)(　　　) (　　　) translator of Japanese literature. He is (4)(　　　) known for his translations of Kawabata, which led to Kawabata winning the Nobel Prize in Literature in (5)(　　　).

GRAMMAR BANK

本文中の下線部(1)と(2)について、86ページの文法解説を参考にそれぞれの指示に従い書き換えなさい。

(1) ①原級を使って　＿＿＿＿＿＿＿＿＿＿＿＿＿＿＿＿
　　②最上級を使って　＿＿＿＿＿＿＿＿＿＿＿＿＿＿＿＿
(2) ①原級を使って　＿＿＿＿＿＿＿＿＿＿＿＿＿＿＿＿
　　②比較級を使って　＿＿＿＿＿＿＿＿＿＿＿＿＿＿＿＿

LESSON 23 　　比 較 (2)

◆ A. 注意すべき比較表現

(1) **原級によるもの**

1. This street is **twice as** wide **as** that one.「...の2倍〜」
2. You must eat **as** slowly **as** you **can**.「できるだけ〜」
   (=You must eat **as** slowly **as possible**.)
3. He is **not so much** a writer **as** a scholar.「AよりむしろB」

(2) **比較級によるもの**

4. She is **the taller of the two**.「2者のうちでより〜な方」
5. He is **less** intelligent **than** his brother.「...ほど〜でない」
   (=He is not as [so] intelligent as his brother.)
6. Cathy is **more** kind **than** gentle.「BよりむしろA」
   　　　　　　　　　　　　　　　〈同一人の異なる性質の比較〉
   Cf. Cathy is kind**er than** the other girls. 〈別人の同じ性質の比較〉
7. The sky was growing **darker and darker**.「だんだん〜」
8. **The harder** you work, **the more** you earn.
   「〜すればするほど、ますます...」
9. A dolphin is **no more** a fish **than** a horse is.
   「Aが〜でないのは、Bが〜でないのと同じ」

(3) **最上級によるもの**

10. **The strongest man** has his weak points.「どんなに〜でも」
11. It was *a* **most** enjoyable evening. (most=very)
12. The lake is **deepest** near the island. 　〈同一物に関する比較〉
    Cf. The lake is **the deepest** of the five. 　〈他との比較〉
13. **Most** animals can be found in the zoo.「たいていの」
14. He has **at least** 300 foreign stamps.「少なくとも」

《チェックテスト23》

次の各文の( )内に適語を補いなさい。
1. You must run as fast as (　　　).
2. He is (　　　) clever than honest.
3. This is a (　　　) amusing story.
4. She is (　　　) shorter of the two.

EXERCISE 23

① 次の各組の文がほぼ同じ意味になるように、(　)内に適語を補いなさい。

1. a. I am not as energetic as you.
   b. I am (　　　) energetic (　　　) you.
2. a. This room is twice the size of that one.
   b. This room is twice (　　　) large (　　　) that one.
3. She is an actress rather than a singer.
   b. She is not (　　　) (　　　) a singer (　　　) an actress.

② 日本文の意味を表すように、次の各文の(　)内に適語を補いなさい。

1. 彼は控えめというよりはむしろ内気だ。
   He is (　　　) shy (　　　) modest.
2. 2つの問題のうち、こちらの方がやさしい。
   This is (　　　) (　　　) of the two problems.
3. 人は年をとればとるほど、おだやかになる。
   The (　　　) we grow, the (　　　) quiet we become.

③ 次の各文の意味を書きなさい。

1. They wanted to get married as soon as they could.

2. Nowadays more and more people are using the Internet.

3. I heard a most interesting talk about superstitions.

4. He feels happiest only when he is talking with her.

5. You must cut the grass at least once a week in summer.

④ 次の各文の(　)内の語を並べ替えて正しい文にしなさい。

1. He (than / less / brother / is / his / active).

2. She (are / than / no / mad / is / more / you).

3. Most (is / that / people / innocent / believe / he).

91

Preservatives

Preservatives have a history (1)<u>as far back as</u> 12,000 B.C. One of (2)<u>the oldest</u> ways to preserve food is to dry it out in the sun. Japanese dry seaweed and eat it with rice. Italians dry tomatoes and eat them (3)<u>later</u> with pasta. Native Americans dried the buffalo meat that they couldn't eat immediately. Now Americans dry beef and sell it as a snack called beef jerky.

A lot of the food that we eat today is preserved. Drying is just one way of keeping food (4)<u>longer</u>. There are many others such as sugaring, smoking, pickling, canning and bottling, and fermenting.

In Europe, cheese is (5)<u>the most popular</u> preserved food. (6)<u>The biggest</u> producer of cheese in Europe is Germany, but France produces (7)<u>the greatest</u> variety of cheeses. Most varieties of cheese are made from cow's milk, but some are made from goat's milk. Jam and smoked sausages are also popular in Europe. Many farmers like to make jam from the fruit they grow, but many people in Britain say that orange marmalade made from Spanish Seville oranges is one of (8)<u>the tastiest</u>.

Japanese preservatives, especially fermented foods, are also becoming (9)<u>more and more popular</u> overseas. For example, you can now buy *miso* at many food markets. Also, vegetarians are fond of eating *natto* and tofu, both made from soybeans. Sushi is probably (10)<u>the most well-known</u> Japanese food. Originally, sushi was fish preserved in rice. It was sold at street stalls in old Edo City. Now there are sushi restaurants all over the world.

NOTES

preservative「保存料、保存法」　　**dry out~**「~を完全に乾燥させる」　　**seaweed**「海苔（のり）、海藻」　　**Native Americans**「アメリカ先住民族」　　**buffalo**「アメリカバイソン」　　**beef jerky**「ビーフジャーキー」（保存用乾燥牛肉）　　**sugar**「砂糖をまぶす」　　**smoke**「燻製にする」　　**pickle**「酢漬けにする」　　**can**「缶詰にする」　　**ferment**「発酵させる」　　**preserved food**「保存食」　　**variety of~**「~の種類」　　**Spanish Seville**「スペインのセビリア（地方の）」　　**tasty (tastier, tastiest)**「おいしい」　　**be fond of** = like　　**soybean**「大豆」　　**stall**「屋台」

STORY BANK

本文の内容と合っているものにはT、間違っているものにはFを書き入れなさい。

(1) (　) Preserving foods has a very long history in Europe, America and Japan.
(2) (　) Italians dry tomatoes and sell them as a kind of snack.
(3) (　) Drying food is the best way to preserve foods in Europe.
(4) (　) Tofu and *natto* are preserved foods, and sushi was also originally a preserved food.

CULTURAL BANK

英文を聞いて空所に適切な語を書き入れなさい。

(1) The word "jerky" in beef jerky came from a Native (　　　　) word which means "dried, salted (　　　　)."
(2) Camembert is the (　　　　) (　　　　) French cheese in Japan, but traditionally, there are from 350 to (　　　　) distinct types of French cheese.
(3) Japanese oranges, or *mikan,* are sometimes called Satsuma. The name (　　　　) (　　　　) the former Satsuma Province from where these fruits were first exported to the (　　　　).
(4) People used to eat sushi at a fashionable sushi (　　　　), now people eat sushi at a sushi-go-round or conveyor belt sushi (　　　　).

GRAMMAR BANK

本文中の下線部(1)~(10)の比較の用法を、90ページの文法解説を参考に、原級、比較級、最上級を使った用法に分類し番号で答えなさい。

1. 原級　＿＿＿＿＿＿＿＿＿＿＿＿＿＿＿＿＿＿＿＿＿
2. 比較級　＿＿＿＿＿＿＿＿＿＿＿＿＿＿＿＿＿＿＿＿＿
3. 最上級　＿＿＿＿＿＿＿＿＿＿＿＿＿＿＿＿＿＿＿＿＿

LESSON 24　　前置詞

◆ A. 基本的用法

1. I met him **at** the bus stop.　〈場所の一点〉
2. The concert began **at** seven.　〈時の一点〉
3. He will be back **in** two hours.　〈時の経過〉
4. The woman **in** white is Martha.　〈着用〉
5. She was born **on** October 5th.　〈曜日・日〉
6. He was standing **by** the gate.　〈近接〉
7. We went to Tokushima **by** ship.　〈手段〉
8. Eggs are sold **by** the dozen.　〈単位〉
9. They left **for** India last week.　〈方向〉
10. France is famous **for** its wine.　〈原因・理由〉
11. I sold the book **for** five dollars.　〈交換〉
12. Mr. Takahashi is **from** Fukuoka.　〈出身〉
13. How far is it **from** here **to** Rome?　〈起点・到着点〉
14. I cut the rope **with** this knife.　〈道具〉

◆ B. 注意すべき前置詞

1. a. We lived there **for** ten years.　〈持続期間〉
   b. We lived there **during** the winter.　〈特定の期間中〉
2. a. Stay here **till** seven o'clock.　〈継続〉
   b. Finish this **by** seven o'clock.　〈期限〉
3. a. This chair is made **of** wood.　〈材料〉
   b. Wine is made **from** grapes.　〈原料〉
4. a. She set the vase **on** the table.　〈接触〉
   b. There is a bridge **over** the river.　〈真上〉
   c. He lifted his hands **above** his head.　〈上方〉

◆ C. 群前置詞 ── 1つの前置詞と同じ働きをする語の集まりをいう。

1. I couldn't sleep **because of** the heat.「～のために」
2. His absence was **due to** the storm.「～のためで」
3. **According to** Alice, he is a good teacher.「～によると」
4. The load was lifted **by means of** a crane.「～によって」
5. She married him **in spite of** my opposition.「～にもかかわらず」

EXERCISE 24

① 次の各文の( )内に、下記の語群から適語を補いなさい。

1. He went out (　　　) a dark suit.
2. I will finish it (　　　) next Wednesday.
3. A jet plane is flying (　　　) the hill.
4. Scotland is famous (　　　) its whisky.
5. The burglar opened the door (　　　) a key.
6. Sydney is about eight miles (　　　) here.
7. She did not come back (　　　) seven o'clock.

[by / for / from / in / over / till / with]

② 次の各文の誤りを正しなさい。

1. Bread is made of flour.

2. There is a mirror on the sink.

3. The meeting lasted in two hours.

③ 次の各文の意味を書きなさい。

1. The baseball game was canceled because of the rain.

2. In spite of a bad storm, the plane landed safely.

3. We got out of the hotel by means of the fire escape.

4. According to the weather report, it will snow tomorrow.

④ 次の各文の( )内の語を並べ替えて正しい文にしなさい。

1. They (next / leave / Taiwan / will / Monday / for).

2. I'll (the / you / museum / meet / at / science).

3. He (again / spite / efforts / of / failed / in / his).

The Tramp

Do you know what a tramp looks like? He is someone who wears dusty old clothes and ill-fitting shoes. He carries a cane or a little umbrella. He sways (1)<u>from</u> right (2)<u>to</u> left as he goes along. He wears a funny little hat and he is the famous Charlie Chaplin.

Charlie Chaplin made the main character in *The Tramp* from clothes that were in a dressing room (3)<u>at</u> a Hollywood studio. "I wanted everything to be a contradiction," he said, so he chose baggy pants, a tight coat, a small hat and large shoes.

The Tramp always makes mistakes and gets into trouble. He is poor and has no home to go to. He is a good-hearted man but he is always unlucky in love. In each movie there is both laughter and tears. The Tramp went on to be an icon of the silent movie era.

Tora-san is often spoken of as being the Charlie Chaplin of Asia. He is the icon of Japan's time of rapid economic growth. He wears a light brown jacket over a light brown, knitted belly warmer. He has *setta* on his feet, and he carries a little suitcase. He walks slowly because he has no place to go in a hurry. He is (4)<u>from</u> Tokyo, but he rarely goes back there. Just like Charlie Chaplin's character, he nearly always falls in love with a pretty lady, but at the end of the movie he has to move on. Each of the 48 movies in the *It's Tough Being a Man* series continues to be popular with all generations.

NOTES

tramp「放浪者」　**ill-fitting**「(体に)ぴったりと合わない」　**sway**「傾く」　**go along**「進む」　**Charlie Chaplin**「チャーリー・チャップリン」(1889~1977)　***The Tramp***『チャップリンの失恋』(映画名)　**dressing room**「楽屋」　**contradiction**「正反対、あべこべ」　**baggy pants**「だぶだぶのズボン」　**good-hearted**「親切な」　**go on ~**「~となる」　**icon**「象徴」　**Tora-san**「フーテンの寅さん」(渥美清1928~1996)　**time of rapid economic growth**「高度経済成長期」　**knitted belly warmer**「毛糸の腹巻」　**move on**「立ち去る」　***It's Tough Being a Man***『男はつらいよ』(映画シリーズ名)

STORY BANK

本文の内容と合っているものにはT、間違っているものにはFを書き入れなさい。

(1) (　) Both Chaplin and Tora-san wear a hat and knitted belly warmers.
(2) (　) Charlie Chaplin himself chose the clothes for the tramp character.
(3) (　) *The Tramp* is a silent movie and ends happily.
(4) (　) Both Chaplin and Tora-san fall in love with a pretty lady in their movies.

CULTURAL BANK

英文を聞いて空所に適切な語を書き入れなさい。

Sir Charles Spencer Chaplin was a British film actor and director who worked mainly (1)(　　　) the U.S. He was involved (2)(　　　) making humorous silent films (3)(　　　) the 1920's. Chaplin wrote, directed, produced, edited, starred in, and composed the music (4)(　　　) most of his films. *The Gold Rush* (1925) and *Limelight* (1952) are two (5)(　　　) his particularly world famous movies.

GRAMMAR BANK

本文中の下線部(1)~(4)の前置詞を、94ページの文法解説を参考に説明しなさい。

(1) _____　(2) _____
(3) _____　(4) _____

LESSON 25　仮定法 (1)

A. 仮定法過去 ── 現在の事実に反する仮定や、現在において実現できない願望を表す。

(1) 仮定を表す場合：「もし (今) 〜なら、...するだろうに」

$$\text{If} + S + \begin{Bmatrix} \text{過去形} \\ \text{were [was《口語》]} \end{Bmatrix} \sim, \; S + \begin{Bmatrix} \text{would, should} \\ \text{could, might} \end{Bmatrix} + \text{原形} \cdots$$

   1. If I **had** wings, I **could fly** to America.
     (=As I don't have wings, I can't fly to America.)

(2) 願望を表す場合：「I wish+S+過去形」の形式を用いる。
　「〜であればよいのに」
   2. **I wish** I **were** ten years younger.
     (=I am sorry I am not ten years younger.)

B. 仮定法過去完了 ── 過去の事実に反する仮定や、過去において実現しなかった願望、または悔恨を表す。

$$\text{If} + S + \text{had} + \text{過去分詞} \sim, \; S + \begin{Bmatrix} \text{would, should} \\ \text{could, might} \end{Bmatrix} + \text{have} + \text{過去分詞} \cdots$$

(1) 仮定を表す場合：「もし (あの時) 〜だったら、...しただろうに」
   1. If I **had taken** an umbrella, I **would not have got** wet.
     (=As I didn't take an umbrella, I got wet.)
     Cf. If you **had** not **followed** his advice, you **would be** dead now.
     (= You aren't dead now because you followed his advice.)

(2) 願望を表す場合：「I wish+S+過去完了形」の形式を用いる。
　「〜であればよかったのに」
   2. **I wish** I **had saved** my money while I was young.
     (=I am sorry I didn't save my money while I was young.)

《チェックテスト25》

次の各文の (　) 内の動詞を適切な形に変えなさい。
1. If I (be) free today, I would go with you.
2. I wish I (know) how to plant young trees.
3. If he (come) earlier, I could have seen him.
4. I wish I (study) harder when I was a student.

EXERCISE 25

⟨1⟩ 次の各文を仮定法を用いて書き換えなさい。

1. I have an engagement, so I cannot see you.

2. I am sorry I am not as intelligent as you.

3. She didn't marry him, so she is not happy now.

4. I am sorry I did not paint the door white.

5. As he wasn't there, he didn't meet with an accident.

⟨2⟩ 次の各文の誤りを正しなさい。

1. I wish he were at my house then.

2. If it had been fine yesterday, I would go fishing.

3. If I had a car, I could have got there in five minutes.

⟨3⟩ 次の各文の意味を書きなさい。

1. If we had had enough time, we would have visited Nikko.

2. I wish I could live in a fine condominium like that.

3. If the earth were the size of a basketball, the moon would be the size of a tennis ball.

⟨4⟩ 次の各文の( )内の語を並べ替えて正しい文にしなさい。

1. I wish (had / a / with / brought / we / map / us).

2. (you / one / yen / if / had / million), what would you buy?

3. If he had taken my advice, (he / be / now / successful / would / a / businessman).

Presenting Successfully

Do you wish you were a good public speaker or presenter? Many people do. Some people start to shake, get sweaty hands, and their minds go blank. Are you like them? Don't worry. It's only natural to get nervous, says Alison Lester in her book, *Present for Success*. If you were feeling confident and relaxed, you would not become so nervous, she says. She suggests that you talk to yourself in a positive way. Also, being active or walking beforehand will help your brain function more smoothly.

Lester says that content and structure are also important. If you were a doctor, you might talk about an illness and its treatment. Think of a story in different parts: the introduction, the villain (the illness), the hero (the treatment), and the result. Having easy-to-understand content in an easy-to-understand structure is key to making a successful speech.

Have you ever prepared a presentation on your home computer, and then forgotten to take your memory stick to the event? (1)"If only I had made it on my laptop, I could have shown my presentation," you might say. Lester warns that nearly every presenter has experienced technical problems. The answer is to make a speech that doesn't need visuals. She says that visual aids should help the speaker, not be an extra problem for him or her.

Finally, Lester tells her readers to look at a video of themselves. Check your body language and facial expressions. Also check your voice. Don't send an audience home saying: (2)"I wish I could have understood her better." Her last piece of advice is: smile.

NOTES

a good public speaker「人前で上手に話す人」　**presenter**「報告者」　**shake**「震える」　**sweaty**「汗ばんだ」　**mind go blank**「頭の中が真っ白になる」　**confident**「自信のある」　**nervous**「神経質な」　**positive**「肯定的な」　**beforehand**「前もって」　**treatment**「治療」　**easy-to-understand**「容易に理解できる」　**home computer**「自宅のパソコン」　**memory stick**「USB記憶装置」　**send an audience home saying~**「聴衆を~と言わせながら家に返す」

STORY BANK

本文の内容と合っているものにはT、間違っているものにはFを書き入れなさい。

(1) (　) When someone becomes nervous in front of people, he or she is not feeling confident but relaxed.
(2) (　) To make a successful speech, you should talk like a doctor.
(3) (　) Many presenters have experienced technical problems such as forgetting to bring the memory stick.
(4) (　) Body language and facial expressions are also important for your presentation.

CULTURAL BANK

 51

英文を聞いて空所に適切な語を書き入れなさい。

Dear brothers and sisters, we must not forget that millions of people are (1)(　　　　　) from poverty and injustice and ignorance. We must not forget that millions of children are (2)(　　　　　) of their schools. We must not forget that our sisters and brothers are (3)(　　　　　) for a bright, peaceful future.

　So let us wage a glorious struggle against illiteracy, poverty and terrorism, let us (4)(　　　　)(　　　　) our books and our pens, they are the most powerful weapons. One child, one teacher, one book and one pen can (5)(　　　　) the world. Education is the only solution. (6)(　　　　　) first.　　　　[Malala's Speech to the U.N. General Assembly, July 2013]

GRAMMAR BANK

本文中の下線部(1)と(2)について、98ページの文法解説Bを参考にそれぞれ指定された語句で始め、英文を完成させなさい。

(1) As _____
(2) I am _____

LESSON 26　仮定法 (2)

A. 仮定法未来 — should または were to によって、未来の起こりそうもない出来事に対する仮定を表す。should は「万一～したら…だろうに」、were to は「かりに～するとしたら…するだろうに」などの意味に用いられる。

$$\text{If} + \text{S} + \begin{Bmatrix} \text{should} \\ \text{were to} \end{Bmatrix} + 原形～,\ \text{S} + \begin{Bmatrix} \text{would, should} \\ \text{could, might} \end{Bmatrix} + 原形…$$

1. If I **should fail**, I **would** [**will**] **try** again.
2. If you **were to attend** the party, what **would** you **wear**?

　　[注] shouldを用いた仮定では、主節にふつうの文や命令文がくることもある：
　　　　If I **should** be late, don't wait for me.

B. if 節のない仮定表現

1. **A close observer** *would notice* the change.
   (=If he were a close observer, *he would notice the change*.)
2. **But for [Without]** his warning, *she would have drowned*.
   (=If it had not been for his warning, *she would have drowned*.)

C. 仮定法を含む慣用表現

1. **It's (high) time** you *had* a haircut.「もう～してよい時だ」
2. I feel **as if** I *were* in my own house.「まるで～かのように」
3. **If only** I *had gone* by taxi!「～でありさえすればなあ」
4. **If it were not for** the sun's light, we *could not live*.「もし～がなければ」
5. **If it had not been for** your advice, I *would have failed*.
   「もし～がなかったら」

《チェックテスト26》

次の各文の(　)内の動詞を適切な形に変えなさい。
1. If anyone (come), tell him I'm out.
2. He treats me as if I (be) his own child.
3. It's high time you (leave) for school.
4. If it (be not) for you, I couldn't do it.

EXERCISE 26

① 次の各組の文がほぼ同じ意味になるように、（　）内に適語を補いなさい。

1. a. She talks just like a grown-up.
   b. She talks (　　　) (　　　) she (　　　) a grown-up.
2. a. A wise man would act differently.
   b. (　　　) (　　　) (　　　) a wise man, he would act differently.
3. a. But for literature, our lives would be as dry as deserts.
   b. If it (　　　) (　　　) (　　　) literature, our lives would be as dry as deserts.

② 日本文の意味を表すように、次の各文の（　）内に適語を補いなさい。

1. 彼女はまるで恐ろしいものを見たような顔つきをしていた。
   She looked as if she (　　　) (　　　) something terrible.
2. 君の結婚のことを聞いたとしたら、彼は驚くだろう。
   If he (　　　) (　　　) of your marriage, he will be surprised.
3. あなたの時を得た救助がなかったら、私は死んでいただろう。
   If it (　　　) (　　　) (　　　) for your timely rescue, I would have died.

③ 次の各文の意味を書きなさい。

1. If the fax machine should fail, call the repair section and wait.

2. It is high time you began to think about your future career.

3. Without his habit of gambling, he would have made a big fortune.

④ 次の各文の（　）内の語を並べ替えて正しい文にしなさい。

1. It's (the / you / for / time / prepared / party).

2. If (her / I / number / only / knew / telephone)!

3. If (not / for / it / your / been / had / help), I would have lost the game.

READING PASSAGE 26

"What if..."

One day, after going with a friend to buy a lottery ticket, I asked my friend, "What would you do if you (1)<u>were to</u> win the jackpot?" She laughed and said, "To begin with, I doubt if that will ever happen, but if I (2)<u>should win</u> a lot of money, I would like to take my Mum and Dad on a trip around the world."

Then she had a question for me. She said it was a question her parents asked her every New Year's Eve. The question was: "If, as of tomorrow, you (3)<u>were to</u> be in charge of this country, what would you change?" I answered immediately, "I would give every jobless person a job!"

My friend looked surprised at my answer so I explained that my brother had just graduated from a college in the States. He got his degree in counseling but couldn't find a job. "The unemployment rate is about 3.5%. But a close observer (4)<u>would</u> notice that it is not a true marker of the employment situation," I told her. "Some companies can't get enough workers, while some fields are overflowing. If only my brother had studied engineering and mathematics, or computer science, he would have a good job now," I said. My parents agreed that if he had not gone abroad, he would probably be working now.

"The job market is always changing. Tell him to keep trying," my friend said. Then she thought for a while and added, "Perhaps it's high time he (5)<u>came</u> back to Japan, and tried to look for work here."

NOTES

what if~「～だとしたらどうなるだろう」　**go with~**「～と一緒に行く」　**lottery ticket**「宝くじ」　**jackpot**「大当たり」　**as of~**「～から」　**in charge of~**「～を管理している」　**unemployment rate**「失業率」　**close observer**「綿密な観察者」　**marker**「指標」　**employment situation**「雇用情勢・状況」　**overflow**「あふれ出る」　**job market**「求人市場」

STORY BANK

本文の内容と合っているものにはT、間違っているものにはFを書き入れなさい。

(1) (　) The author actually won the lottery and took her parents on a trip.
(2) (　) The author says if she wins the jackpot, she will give every jobless person a job.
(3) (　) The author's brother did not go to America to study counseling.
(4) (　) The unemployment rate alone does not tell us accurately about the unemployment situation.

CULTURAL BANK　　CD 53

英文を聞いて空所に適切な語を書き入れなさい。

(1) (　　　　) is like a lottery. This means that life can be full of uncertainties and (　　　　).
(2) New Year's resolutions are special promises to oneself; like (　　　　) weight or (　　　　) smoking.
(3) In Japan, unemployment compensation is a sum of (　　　　) paid regularly by the government to an unemployed (　　　　).
(4) Counseling as a (　　　　) is the act of listening to people's problems and giving them (　　　　).

GRAMMAR BANK

本文中の下線部(1)～(5)の仮定法の用法を、例のように102ページの文法解説を参考に説明しなさい。

(1) ___仮定法未来___　(2) _____　(3) _____
(4) _____　(5) _____

TEXT PRODUCTION STAFF

edited by
Kenji Matsumoto
Kimio Sato

編集
松本 健治
佐藤 公雄

English-language editing by
Bill Benfield

英文校閲
ビル・ベンフィールド

cover design by
Lighthouse Co., Ltd.

表紙デザイン
株式会社ライトハウス

text design by
Ruben Frosali

本文デザイン
ルーベン・フロサリ

CD PRODUCTION STAFF

narrated by
Katie Adler (AmE)
Bill Sullivan (AmE)

吹き込み者
ケイティー・アドラー（アメリカ英語）
ビル・サリバン（アメリカ英語）

New English Master
リーディングにつなげる英文法

2016年1月20日　初 版 発 行
2025年3月30日　第 7 刷 発 行

著　者　北山 長貴
　　　　Margaret Yamanaka
　　　　福井 慶一郎

発行者　佐野 英一郎

発行所　株式会社 成美堂
　　　　〒101-0052　東京都千代田区神田小川町3-22
　　　　TEL 03-3291-2261　FAX 03-3293-5490
　　　　https://www.seibido.co.jp

印刷・製本　倉敷印刷(株)

ISBN 978-4-7919-4788-1　　　　　　　　　　Printed in Japan

・落丁・乱丁本はお取り替えします。
・本書の無断複写は、著作権上の例外を除き著作権侵害となります。